Young Children Learning

Young Children Learning

Exploration and Language

Alice Yardley

Principal Lecturer in Education,
Nottingham College of Education

Citation Press · New York · 1973

Published by Evans Brothers Limited
Montague House, Russell Square, London, W.C.1

Citation Press, Library and Trade Division, Scholastic Magazines, Inc.
50 West 44th St., New York, New York 10036

The following are the four titles in the
YOUNG CHILDREN LEARNING series by Alice Yardley:

REACHING OUT
EXPLORATION AND LANGUAGE
DISCOVERING THE PHYSICAL WORLD
SENSES AND SENSITIVITY

Also by Alice Yardley:
THE TEACHER OF YOUNG CHILDREN
YOUNG CHILDREN THINKING

Library of Congress Catalog Card Number: 72-95335
Standard Book Number: 590-07330-3

Cover photograph: Henry Grant, AIIP

Printed in Great Britain by T. and A. Constable Ltd.,
Hopetoun Street, Edinburgh.

PRA 3179

LB
1139
.L3
Y3
1973

Contents

	Introduction	7
1	Experience into words	9
2	The development of speech	15
3	How words acquire meaning	21
4	Communication	26
5	Man's use of symbols	32
6	Words and thought	38
7	Words and personality	44
8	Playing with symbols	50
9	The child's speech	56
10	Words in use	62
11	The importance of literacy	68
12	The child's home background	73
13	How children meet words in their environment	79
14	Listening and speaking	84
15	Becoming familiar with words on paper	91
16	The joy of reading	101
17	The literary value of books available	106
18	Imaginative writing	113
19	Helping the child to become literate	123
20	Problems associated with the teaching of reading	132
	Conclusion: parents and teachers	143
	Suggestions for further reading	145
	Index	149

Figure references in the text indicate particular books in the Suggestions for further reading.

Introduction

In this book language is considered as an aspect of the total development of the child, and the way in which a child learns to use his mother tongue is viewed as a living experience and never as a subject taught. The emphasis is on learning by using; English is not seen simply as a skill to be practised but as a power which binds the child's world together. Although the recognition of words in the form of reading and the use of words on paper in the form of creative writing are given due attention, they are treated as part of a versatile power to communicate which enables the child both to develop the world of his mind and to experience his real world.

This is not a book about the teaching of reading or the development of speech or the acquisition of skill in original writing. It is a book about a gift peculiar to man, about his ability to abstract, to symbolise, to create a world of imagination from the material he garners through his experience of things and situations.

Exploring his world leads to the development of language, and in man's use of symbols his understanding of his world is clearly perceived. The early stages in the development of this understanding are examined and appraised in this book about the child and his words.

Alice Yardley

A note on First Schools and Middle Schools

In the Plowden Report, published in 1967, a change of terminology was introduced amongst recommendations for a revised structure for primary education. The terms 'first school' for the five-to-eight age-group and 'middle school' for the eight-to-twelve were suggested.

At the time of writing, some local authorities are considering a three-tier system with breaks at either eight and twelve or nine and thirteen. Other authorities show little inclination to make any major changes and seem likely to retain breaks at seven and eleven and to continue using the terms 'Infant' and 'Junior' for their Primary schools. In general there is a trend towards a more flexible system, but the final pattern is not yet clear.

Whatever terms are used, the education of young children should be thought of in terms of stages rather than ages, and where the term 'Infant School' appears in this book, it is used only as the label for a school in which young children learn. Examples illustrating points made in the book refer to children whose chronological ages range from birth to about seven or eight years, and they indicate a stage in development rather than the achievement of a particular age-group.

1

Experience into words

Perhaps the most significant event in a child's life occurs at about the age of twelve months. He utters his first word intentionally and with meaning. His parents greet the event with great delight, for they know that their child is acquiring his most important means of understanding. From now on words will provide him with a highly effective medium of communication, and through using words he will become increasingly conscious of his surroundings and of himself.

Man is a social being and needs to communicate. He communicates mostly by using language, and words are the most important units of language. Man alone knows how to use words. They give him power over his environment and enable him to manipulate other people. He values them as unique and powerful tools, and prizes them above his other gifts.

In our society the articulate person leads. He influences the minds of others, and the highly articulate person inspires reverence and sometimes fear in his colleagues. His very competence may render others inarticulate and make them feel inadequate. Our civilisation is shaped and held together by words. If words were taken away, the world as we know it would disintegrate. Skill in the acquisition and use of words is the prime aim of education in the schools.

On entering school at the age of five, Celia appeared to be perfectly normal. She was an attractive girl with pretty hair, a delicate skin and large luminous grey eyes. She made no attempt to take part in what was happening. She made no response when spoken to. She just sat, her grey eyes giving nothing away as they followed the activities of the children round her. After two weeks the teacher became worried by her refusal to speak. She fetched Celia's seven-year-old sister, June, to confirm that Celia could, in fact, speak. 'Oh, she knows,' June assured the teacher. 'She's always been shy.'

Eventually the teacher learned that Celia was the youngest of a family of five girls whose ages ranged from Celia aged five to Patsy aged eighteen. Celia, with four little 'mothers' besides her adult mother, found most of her needs anticipated and satisfied without being forced to express them. When she entered school she lacked the normal means of learning. It was difficult to assess her understanding and impossible to estimate her mental powers. It took the years of the Infant School to encourage her to communicate adequately with others. Throughout her school career her handicap was enormous. Her ability to cope with the literate world she inherited was severely impaired.

When we listen to the skilled oratory of a Prime Minister or an archbishop, when we are moved by the words of a play, when we hear the incessant chatter of people round us, it is difficult to realise that so many words – and ways of using them – originated in the baby's first simple sounds. The baby's first cry becomes a means of communicating his needs to someone who responds. From his first breath the baby utters simple sounds, and the long and complicated process of learning about words and growing into the use of them has begun. The drive which forces the child to accomplish speech is founded in his need to survive.

If the child is to learn how to live in the world, he must make sense of his surroundings. His natural curiosity moves him to explore. For the first year or so he must do this without words. He cannot depend on being told what to do, he must rely on his own resources. It is through his sensory experiences and the emotions associated with them that he collects and retains information. In other parts of this series (*Reaching Out*, Chapter 3, and *Discovering the Physical World*) we consider in some detail the way in which a child gains his knowledge of the world. Here we shall concern ourselves primarily with the way in which he organises this information.

As the number of his experiences increases, the baby becomes aware that groups of experiences have something in common. He comes to appreciate connections between this and that and he learns to discriminate between them. Perceiving differences helps him to perceive likenesses. Eventually the essence of what is similar emerges in the form of an idea and at a later stage the adult gives him a word to which he recognises his idea can be attached. He will continue to associate further similar experiences with the word idea, and so the map of his mind begins to take shape.

Meaning at this stage is embodied in sensory and emotional experience, and the ultimate quality of his thought as an adult is founded on such sensory comprehension. Meaning leads to understanding and these together provide the foundation of the child's intellectual development. Examination of a few of the child's elementary ideas will illustrate this point and show how the words a child uses with meaning represent his understanding of his experiences.

Amongst the baby's basic speech patterns can be heard the 'ma-ma', 'da-da' sounds, and babies in every country utter these sounds, irrespective of the mother tongue they will later learn. From her first days Wendy's parents talked to her. Sometimes her mother would sing to her and clap her little hands together, using such words as, 'Clap hands, clap hands till Daddy comes home'. When only a few months old Wendy would rock and croon when she heard her mother singing.

When she was uncomfortable or hungry, she would murmur 'mum-mum' to herself and this usually meant that she was miserable. At four months old she would utter 'mum-mum', or 'mam-mam', or 'dad-dad' quite clearly without associating the sounds with a specific person, object or situation. A few weeks later she would sometimes utter these sounds with pleasure, as though she enjoyed making the sound and hearing herself make it.

By the time she was six months old she would call 'mam-mam', 'dad-dad' when she was wet or unhappy. When Mother had attended to her and spoken words of comfort, Wendy would repeat the 'mam-mam' sound, as though in gratitude. She was nearly seven months old when she began to associate 'dad-dad' with her father and utter the sound as an intelligible word when he attended to her.

Meanwhile her mother helped her to associate the 'mam-mam' sound with herself by talking to her: 'Come to mam-mam!' 'Ma-ma can hear you.' 'There! Ma-ma has made you clean again.' By about seven and a half months Wendy was using the 'mam-mam' sound in response to her mother.

Wendy was by now well aware of her own utterances. They emerged from her as part of her physical state and she associated both sensory and emotional feeling with them. The soft warmth and comfort of her mother's body, the distress she felt when hungry and the satisfaction of having her hunger appeased, the soothing assurance of her mother's voice were all part of her use and recognition of the 'mam-mam' sound. The 'dad-dad' sound she associated with more exciting, vigorous experiences, particularly with clapping and jogging up and down.

In later life the word 'mother' or 'father' would represent all these early experiences she associated with it, together with experiences she acquired during childhood. In adult life the word 'mother' can represent warmth, comfort, satisfaction and frustration. For less fortunate people, it can represent neglect, harshness and even fear. The meaning an individual associates with a word depends on his unique experiences, and meaning varies widely between people.

In a similar way, a number of words are grafted on to basic speech patterns, but the adult gives the child many words which are not directly linked with these basic forms. Some of these will be considered in Chapter 3.

When the child begins to name things, he has begun to impose order on his environment. The name 'rattle', for instance, stands for a group of experiences which have a common quality. This is classification. Grouping and classification lead to generalising, or abstracting that which holds these experiences together as a class. The name doesn't necessarily stand for any single idea but rather for the idea of all similar ideas. Thus the word 'rattle' stands for the idea which all rattles have in common. It defines an object with certain limited characteristics and which obeys certain limited rules. When using it the child has pooled a number of sense impressions. His sense impressions have grown into clear ideas. The quality of these ideas depends on the intensity and variety of the experiences which preceded them and with which they will continue to be associated.

At quite an early age the child begins to recognise the power of words. He utters an anguished 'mam-mam' and his mother appears. By using the word 'ballie' in an appealing tone he can persuade even the stranger to pick up his ball and give it to him every time he throws it over the pram. The word 'No!' has tremendous possibilities.

As the child grows older and more articulate he finds in words a means of extending his exploration of the world, and between the ages of three and six he will pester attentive adults with questions. At a later stage he will seek his answers in books.

At all stages words offer the child opportunity and pleasure. He has every encouragement to develop his skill in using them.

The complexities of becoming familiar with his mother tongue are conquered even by the child with little intelligence. Nearly all forms of human activity will involve him in words, and if he fails to acquire them he fails as a human being. Few people fail in the early stages while learning language is part of living. It is later, when language is sometimes taught as a subject or attempts are made to isolate the study of it, that failure appears.

2

The development of speech

People communicate with one another in many ways: by facial expression and miming, by writing and speaking, by pictures, signs and diagrams and through the modes of expression employed in art. Most forms of communication involve the use of symbols, or vehicles expressing thoughts and feelings. By using symbols we are able to exchange ideas and impressions. While we are unable to transfer our ideas, we can at least convey information about them. Man alone is able to do this.

Speech is the most widely used form of language and words are the units with which speech is structured. Words only become speech when they have meaning and stand for the objects they represent and when they are spoken so that they are comprehensible to others.[1] The first noises a baby makes become speech when they are used to symbolise, when they are made intentionally and with meaning, and when they are understood by another person.

The baby is born with functioning speech organs: he cries, he babbles, and his vocal sounds are accompanied by gestures. He will only develop the use of speech, however, if he is reared amongst people who speak. He will acquire the language of those who speak to him.

Under normal circumstances a child learns to speak in the

home. His ability to learn and the quality of his learning throughout his life depend considerably on the speech education he receives from his family. Most parents realise this and give the baby all the help they can. Fortunately they expect the child to accomplish speech naturally, and therefore they avoid hampering the child by their anxiety at this stage. Their faith in their child's ability to learn to speak is his greatest aid.

We will go back to Wendy and see what else was happening between her and her parents. From birth she was spoken to frequently during feeding, bathing, and so on. When she showed signs of trying to respond or imitate, single words or phrases were repeated. Her mother said, 'She is allowed to put her fingers on our lips as we talk when she wants to as we feel it all helps her. Rhymes and nursery songs are often sung. She rocks and claps her hands and we joggle her up and down.'

Sometimes Wendy would babble to herself. She seemed to listen to the sound she made and then repeat it. 'Dad . . . dad . . . Mam . . . mam . . . Nan . . . nan.' She would smile and wave her arms and legs in pleasure. She would respond with a smile when her mother spoke to her or even when she heard her mother's voice.

Following her use of the words 'dad-dad' and 'mam-mam', she added to her vocabulary 'wow-wow' at nine months, 'd'tee' (dirty) also at nine months, and at ten months 'dodee' (dolly) and 'teddy'.

Sometimes these sounds were muddled unless an adult said the correct word first. Then she would correct herself in imitation. By this time she understood many things which were said to her and would respond to suggestions such as 'Go and find your dolly'. Later she would find things which were not in view.

She was nearly a year old before she added any new 'words' to her vocabulary, but her passive (or understood) vocabulary had greatly increased by this time. It was as though she were consolidating what she had already learned. Much of her effort at this time went into standing and walking. Once these skills were accomplished her range of exploration was widened and her speech began to develop quickly.

She showed great interest in sounds of all descriptions. Listening to the clock she would say, 'dee-dee'. She liked to blow a recorder and make sounds such as 'Bmm, click, yum-yum'. 'Mew' was adopted as the name of the cat, in spite of her parents' use of 'Pussy'.

By twelve months Wendy, an intelligent child with understanding parents, had established a foundation of sound patterns on which her speech could grow. Not only was she able to express her needs and show her approval to those who relieved them, she could use her speech sounds for pleasure. Learning her mother tongue gave her great delight.

Wendy's relationship with her parents was an important feature of her developing speech. They provided her with a pattern she could imitate; they tried to link her mind with theirs, and they shared the experience of speech with her and made it one she delighted in sharing.

Nicholas is barely seven weeks old. Already he opens his mouth when his mother speaks to him. When she stops speaking he utters an encouraging crooning sound until she speaks again. He smiles when she laughs and speaks. Young as he is he seems to strive after speech. The emphasis is where it should be. The child is striving to accomplish a skill. His parents are trying to help him to do what *he* wants to do, rather than force on him something they want him to do. The whole experience is a great joy to all who participate.

The importance of the child's relationship with his parents cannot be overestimated. Where speech is concerned, the mother in particular plays a leading role. Children brought up in a normal family with a single mother figure appear to benefit. Institutionalised children tend to speak later, in spite of the loving devotion of the adults who rear them. The child brought up by the middle-class mother would seem to be in the best situation. The lower-working-class mother tends to express her feelings in non-verbal terms by using a hug or a shove in place of speech, and so little pressure is placed on the child to verbalise.

From the moment of birth, the middle-class mother maintains a constant and close relationship with her baby. She uses every possible means of communicating with him and encourages him in his endeavour to communicate by trying to understand and respond to his signals. She provides him with good word patterns. She uses well-constructed sentences when she speaks. Her voice modulates to convey meaning. Listening to her is a pleasure. She is patient with her child when he strives towards adult speech. In her well-equipped home she has often more time to listen to him than has the mother who is striving against overwhelming odds to cater for a large family.

A baby understands many of the things said to him by people he knows well long before he uses intelligible words. Many infants will try to utter a series of sounds in imitation of sentence patterns before they say single words. Michael, aged twelve months, sat on his father's knee in the bus. He jabbered with great delight and his father responded as though holding a conversation. Mother asked in some surprise, 'Can you tell what he says? I can't.' 'Neither can I,' Father admitted. 'But he wants you to answer him, so I do.'

This kind of attention on the part of the adult affords the child the best possible encouragement. The over-attentive adult, however, can hinder the development of speech. If a child's needs are too often anticipated, he is not forced to express them. The child must need to verbalise and then earn the reward of adult understanding if he is to strive after speech.

Another important factor in speech development is the example of speech which surrounds the child. The child who hears conversation between his parents and other members of his family has something to imitate. His ability to say words is a skill which develops naturally in him, but his skill can only be exercised if his environment offers him the appropriate material.

Like other aspects of the child's development, speech follows an ordered pattern. All children go through the same sequence of stages, but the rate and quality of learning vary from child to child. In the early months of life the baby communicates by means of crying, gesture, and simple sounds which later become babbling. Crying and gestures enable him to communicate in a primitive way until his speech has developed. Babbling provides exercise for the organs of speech, and the physical ability to produce sounds and combine them is present long before a child is mentally ready. The association of meaning with word patterns must be present before we can use the term speech for the sounds made by the child. The child has still to learn how to arrange his words into groups, or sentences, before he can communicate adequately.

Children are good imitators. The child catches his speech from the people he hears. A good model is essential and the child will try hard to imitate faithfully. Much of what he hears reaches his ears as a blurred, undulating pattern of sound. The child needs the help of an adult if he is to learn to articulate correctly. Twins or children born close together tend to speak poorly, because they spend much time speaking to one another and their model is poor.[2] The mature speech of the adult is essential as a good example.

When Judith was nearly two, her German cousin Johann, also two, came to live with her parents. The two children seemed to get on with one another and played together for much of their waking time. Each tried to imitate the other and eventually they created a unique language which each understood but which remained almost completely unintelligible to adults round them. It wasn't until they went to school and made independent friends that this language was abandoned and Johann learned to speak English.

Once a child has learned to speak he can communicate with others and, equally important, he can communicate with himself. As adults we usually do this inwardly, but the young child will often talk to himself aloud. He is equally happy to talk to inanimate objects.

When she was nearly two, Kathy's parents moved to a new bungalow. During the first few days Kathy spent much time by herself, trotting from door to door in the hall and pointing: 'Atta cakie.' (That is the kitchen, i.e. where I have a cake.) 'Atta keen a teet.' (That is the bathroom where I clean my teeth.) 'Atta Kakie ded.' (That is Kathy's bedroom.) 'Atta Mam-mam.' (That is mother's bedroom.) She was identifying familiar landmarks in her new home by naming them to herself.

In a good home children are encouraged to chatter. When possible they are included in adult conversation. They are talked to and listened to and parents know intuitively that this early chatter is the basis of learning. When the child enters school his opportunities for chatter are extended. Modern infant teachers no longer consider the silent classroom to be a symbol of good control and their children are no longer denied their most effective means of discovering, through speech, what the world and the people who live in it are about.

3

How words acquire meaning

Sound patterns only become words when they have meaning. Words can be articulated without becoming part of speech. We can train a parrot to articulate, but only man can fill these sounds with meaning. Human speech is the unification of thought and sound, and in meaning we see the relationship between thought and speech.

The child has to learn to attach meaning to words. Furthermore, he has to learn that not only must a word mean something to him but the meaning he associates with it must be much the same as the meaning other people associate with the same word. A child will be brought up amongst people whose experiences are similar to his own. As a result his concepts and the words which symbolise them will be similar to those of the people with whom he communicates. The policeman's son, for instance, will attach particular meaning to the term 'beat'.

Saying a word is only a stage in the child's growing awareness. The use of a vocal symbol crystallises experience and thought, but the ultimate meaning attached to that symbol is not limited to what the child understands when he first uses it. Further experience, and reflection on experience, will continue to enrich the word with further meaning.

Consider the word 'blanket', for instance. The baby in his pre-speech stages knows a good deal about his blanket. He knows the comforting warmth of it round him and the distressing cold if it falls away. He knows its roughness against his tongue and the queer smell of it when he has sucked it. He learns to recognise it under different guises. It can be pink or blue, big and thick or thin and light. Other people use blankets. There is a huge one when he goes into bed beside mother and father.

At a certain stage in his understanding the word 'blanket' attaches itself to all these different experiences. He may recognise the spoken word 'blanket' as meaning all of these things, even before he utters the sound himself. He is led through meaning to the word.

Once he has acquired the word in speech it stands for his experiences and becomes verbal thought. But saying the word 'blanket' is neither the beginning nor the end of knowing it, for meaning will be added as he meets blanket in fresh situations. As adults, for example, we now know electric blankets and Acrilan and Courtelle blankets. As long as we live we get to know more about the words we already use, and the words we use link us with early experience.

When a child first uses a word in speech the meaning he associates with it may be very limited. At eleven months Wendy associated 'baby' with a picture on a cereal packet. Soon she began to associate 'baby' with any picture of people and with herself. This was a very happy experience. Supported by mother's delight in her achievement, she proceeded to say 'baby' for every object, even those she had already named.

At about the same time, Wendy was brought face-to-face with another child of the same age. She touched it and called it 'baby'. She seemed to expect it to behave like her reflection in the mirror. When it began to babble independently, she was frightened and pulled away.

At twelve months Wendy used the word 'truck' for her own wooden truck but not for the wooden truck belonging to another child. Eight months later, she used the word 'two' for her own two shoes. After that she called any group of objects 'two'.

When a child comes into school he has acquired a vocabulary of about 10,000 words.[3] He will double this before he leaves the Infant School. He has picked up these words from adults and will start to use them as soon as he can attach any meaning to them. He can't wait until he has acquired the adult range of their meaning. It is very easy to assume that if a child uses a word correctly in a particular situation he has grasped the full range of its meaning.

A child may use such mathematical terms as 'fast' and 'slow', associating speed with them. Talking to him about speed soon reveals the fact that for him the word 'speed' means 'going fast like we do on the motorway'. It may have something to do with the shape of a speed car, but he is quite unable to connect it with his idea of slow. He has no concept at all of velocity.

When he uses the word 'round' he means round like a ball. He has yet to learn that it can mean round like a penny or a cocoa-tin, that the equator goes round the world, and that when we 'round off' an object we make it smooth, and, later still, that a 'round dozen' means full.

In one Infant School a group of six-year-old children were interested in shapes. Material provided by the teacher helped to extend this interest and the children were awakened to the shape of the things they handled. One child brought a huge tricorn shell. It was filthy and had been lost amongst the rubbish in the attic since his father brought it back from the war. The interest in shape in the school had helped the child to recognise its possibilities.

The boy washed his shell and polished it. He felt its hardness. His fingers slipped inside the smooth hollow. 'It must be lovely to live inside there,' he murmured. 'It would keep all the sea out.' Then he enjoyed the design on the shell. With his finger he traced the curling pattern. 'It goes round and round and round until it gets to nothing at the top,' he reflected.

4

Communication

Important as speech is, we must remember that it is not the only means of communicating thoughts and emotions. The child's education must include a wide variety of ways in which he can express his experiences, convey his impressions to others, and interpret the modes of expression used by other people.

The new-born baby depends considerably on crying as a means of expressing and conveying his needs and reactions. The baby's first cry assures us that he can breathe. He continues to cry, but his crying diminishes as his powers of speech develop. Crying is common to all babies and wherever they are born in the world they cry in the same way.

While parents expect their baby to cry, his crying often worries them, not so much because the sound is annoying as because it distresses them. Crying is associated with pain and unhappiness, and is often regarded as purely childish behaviour. Adults in our society, particularly male adults, are expected to avoid the use of tears to express feeling.

Parents respond to the expressive cries of their baby, and it is from this simple beginning that he learns to use vocal sounds, and later speech, as one means of communicating. But the baby of even a few weeks old uses other ways of making his needs known, such as wriggling when he is wet or smacking his lips when he is hungry, and if these signs are understood by his parents he will reserve his crying for more desperate situations.

Facial expressions and gestures accompany crying, but may be used independently. Again from such simple beginnings we get mime, sign-language, and the drama and dance of adult life. In ballet we find an artistic synthesis of all these forms of communication. When we watch a play or an opera, it is difficult for us to realise that all of this originated in the elementary movements and calls of the baby.

By the time the child enters school he is using most of the modes of communication available to man. Much of his time in school will be spent in developing these skills. We cannot develop the child's skill with words effectively if we neglect other aspects of his language development, and when we foster his use of many modes of expression we find that they all contribute to his verbal skill.

Very often we find that words permeate even his physical and artistic forms of language. An observer in an Infant School is struck by the diversity and skill of the six-year-old child in his use of communication and by the many aspects of his person that are employed in his exchanges with others.

One of the happiest sounds in the world is the uninhibited laughter of children. It is also highly expressive. It can range from the wicked glee of the child who has caused a flood in the cloakroom by blocking the toilet with soil to the sheer delight of the boy who has created a rainbow with the aid of a spray attached to a hose on a sunny day. A school for young children which rings with merriment is a place of active discovery and emotional satisfaction.

Sometimes the voices of the six-year-old children are silent. Their teacher is telling a story. She watches the faces of the children gathered at her feet. She knows that John understands the humour, that Peggy is identifying with the heroine, that George is puzzled because the story is a little beyond him, that Tina enjoys the thrill of fear, and that Ian's imagination has caught him up in a world beyond the sound of her words. The six-year-old child has not learned to dissemble and all he feels is conveyed by the expression on his face.

Brian and Keith are building with bricks. They rarely speak as the edifice grows between them. Brian is the mastermind. He points and nods or frowns. Sometimes he snatches a brick impatiently. Keith watches and responds. Occasionally he pushes a brick forward tentatively, changing the shape of things, and gurgles with delight if Brian accepts the suggestion.

Play is well under way in the Wendy House. Jill has fetched a scarf from the dressing-up corner. She ties it round her head and parades up and down with a basket, peddling imaginary pegs from door to door. She pauses by the pram and, with fingers arched like claws and her face screwed into a wizened leer, she casts a spell upon the babe.

Outside on the grass a number of children are moving in response to their individual use of percussion instruments. Peter with the castanets matches the sounds he makes with sharp, angular movements of his arms and legs and body. Dawn clashes the cymbals and leaps with the sound. Jenny has a musical box and her dance patterns are complicated as she weaves in circles round the box on the ground. Each child expresses in his own way the feeling stimulated by his own percussion sounds.

One group of children are making books at the writing-table. Very few words appear in the books, but a reader is left in no doubt as to what the child wants to say. Vicki's book, 'My Family', conveys in vivid pictures exactly what she feels about her mother who smokes and has blackened teeth, her father who takes her to play on the swings in the park and Uncle George who is drawn with two heads because 'Mother says he is double-faced'.

Four children at another table are using fabric, feathers and sequins with which to convey their impression of 'what the Queen looks like when she goes to Canada'. Thoughtful Julie has given her a tiny red velvet wrist-bag 'to carry pennies in for the "Ladies" ', and we realise her limited concept of the life of a queen.

John has a lump of clay. He pounds it relentlessly into a pancake and then proceeds to poke his fingers into the pliant surface. Quickly he destroys his pattern and squeezes the lump until his knuckles whiten. His teeth are clenched and we sense the powerful feelings which possess him. Eventually his fingers begin to stroke and smooth the emerging shape of a chubby puppy. With infinite care he details the eyes and the mouth, and then sits back in silent delight and stares at what he has made. He finds something of himself expressed by the clay he has fashioned.

In schools where children are encouraged to live rich and varied lives, expressive behaviour is well developed and highly eloquent. Words may play a subsidiary or primary part, but they are not used in isolation. The child's use of speech is thus enriched and his words are embodied in all he experiences. The child cannot acquire skill in his use of words if they are isolated and dealt with in the form of 'speech training', drill in recognising words in print, spelling lists, and the like. Long before the child can benefit from systematic teaching in word usage, he must develop his natural skill in communication. School offers the child the unique opportunity to communicate with other children and with adults who belong to the world outside his family.

Many of our children come into school with very inadequate modes of expression. The exchange of words in conversation is something they may never experience in the home. In the liberal atmosphere of a modern Infant School children are encouraged to talk to one another as often as to the teacher. Indeed, school is a place where children should do far more talking than the teacher. It is here that many of our children learn to converse through their exchanges with their friends.

Susie, aged five, is wearing a new dress made of pretty blue cotton with crisp white frills. She is anxious to secure the attention of her friend, Jane.

Susie: 'I've got a new dress. My Mum made it. The frills took hours and hours and she says it looks 'spensive.'

Jane: 'What's "'spensive"?'

Susie: ' 'Spensive . . . 'spensive . . . Well, it's posh and she didn't get it from Marks.'

Jane: 'My Mum's got lots and lots of dresses. She goes out when I've gone to bed. She goes dancing and she looks like those dancing ladies on telly.'

Susie: 'I don't care about your Mum. I've got a new dress and I'm going to show it to Miss B [teacher].'

Listening to this exchange of words, one could scarcely call it conversation. Each child is pursuing her own line of thought with little reference to what the other is thinking. These children are highly egocentric in their behaviour and the social graces have yet to develop.

Roy is six and a half. He rushes into school and seeks out his friend, Andrew, with great excitement.

'Our Mike [his big brother] gave me a bob for cleaning his bike. So I'd enough money and I've been to Woollies and got a battery. We can fix that robot with eyes that light up.'

Andrew catches Roy's enthusiasm. 'Super! We'll get that wire stuff from the make-box and we'll ask Miss B for some bulbs.'

While these two boys are working together on their robot, their verbal exchange is interlaced with a number of other forms of communication.

'These bulbs have to fit in here.' Roy wiggles them into sockets (bulb-holders) fixed in their cardboard box robot. They won't stay in place.

'Here!' Andrew has a go. He uses a scrap of adhesive tape. 'There!' He looks to Roy for approval and is rewarded with a grin. 'They'll work like this.' Andrew dramatises a robot. He glides along the floor and indicates with his fingers how the eyes will flash. He returns to the cardboard model and stares from the bulbs to the battery. 'Can you fix the wire?' he asks Roy.

Roy assumes the attitude of the expert and Andrew stands by full of confidence. The bulbs flicker and Andrew thumps Roy on the back. In silence they work together. Andrew obliges by holding bulb-holders and pieces of wire, while Roy fiddles expertly. Glancing at Roy's face from time to time Andrew anticipates his friend's needs and the job is completed. The master-minds now carry their robot from room to room so that all shall appreciate its flashing eyes. Outbursts of dramatic action greet the robot and 'They must be exterminated', 'We must be vitalised,' ring out all over the school.

Many forms of communication are employed in activities of this kind. Children who know one another well will paint a picture together, share the construction of models, or weave a pattern in dance together. Sometimes not a word is spoken. The medium itself provides a channel through which they can share a common experience.

Like other aspects of learning at this stage, communication is a total experience. By encouraging the child to use language in all its diversified forms we foster the full development of each mode of communication for his later use.

5

Man's use of symbols

The child inherits a world where symbols of all kinds play a leading part. Man uses a wide range of symbols and everyday life depends on the individual's skill in using them. In sharing the world of his parents, the child meets these symbols and sees his parents using them wherever he goes and whatever he does.

Man uses maps and diagrams, pictures and photographs, road signs and signals, notes and numbers and words, morse code and other forms of sign language, models and braille, toys, patterns, plans, hand-signals. He also uses many artistic forms of symbolism in the shape of dance, drama, story, and so on.

Man reduces his world to a form of shorthand by making simple signs stand for the real thing. His symbols are convenient and more easily handled than objects and the experiences they represent. While symbols serve man's purposes, they frequently do him a disservice. They can be misinterpreted, and this leads to confusion. Sometimes they are misleading. A boy of seven seeing a live cow for the first time gasped: 'I never thought cows were that big.' Two-dimensional paper pictures are poor substitutes for a living animal.

When we use a symbol it reminds us of a previous experience. We recall things and situations, or feelings which are no longer there. By so doing we can make use of previous experience in a new situation. This is the foundation of reasoning and problem-solving, a means by which we can apply what we have learned to help us to adjust to a fresh set of circumstances.

We begin to develop this skill at a very early age. The baby of five or six months will watch his mother hide his ball under a cushion, and although he cannot see it he will feel under the cushion and retrieve the ball with a squeal of delight. He can use a mental image as a substitute for the real thing.

Michael was two and a half when his aunt fetched him from home to take him out. At the door Michael stopped and asked: 'Is it a long way?' His aunt nodded. 'Yes,' she explained. 'We're going to see Grandma. We shall go on the bus.' Michael let go of her hand. He ran back to the kitchen, opened the pantry door, cut a slice from the chocolate cake on the shelf and wrapped it in a paper napkin. Last time he'd been taken to Grandma's on the bus he'd felt hungry before he arrived. He was using past experience not merely to solve an immediate problem but to anticipate a possible emergency and solve it in advance.

No doubt at this stage Michael's experiences were stored in his mind in the shape of images as much as in words. As his use of words increased he learned to rely more on verbal symbols than on pictorial ones. As adults we solve many problems by talking them out to ourselves.

When we use a symbol we do not need to recall, one by one, all the experiences which gave that symbol meaning. We can step straight on from the stage that symbol represents. Take the case of the word 'bottle'. Long before we recognised the word we had been gathering experiences to provide it with meaning. We knew the banana-shaped bottle from which we first sucked milk. After that stage the milk came in a straight-shaped container. We knew the hard, smooth feel of glass, the warmth of it full of milk, and the satisfaction of the sweet milk filling an empty stomach. On mother's dressing-table there were other kinds of bottles containing a number of things. Father had his collection of bottles in a cupboard. The milkman's bottles were different again and in the chemist shop were bottles of many colours, shapes and sizes. The hot-water bottle and the bottled gas we also knew. Now when we say the word 'bottle' or see a printed word-pattern 'bottle' we know that it represents the characteristics common to all bottles. We have learned to extract those features which all bottles have in common. This process of abstraction leads to an idea and the bottle symbol reminds us of our idea. We can use our idea without referring back to all the bottles we have met. It is on such mental activities that understanding is based and intellect develops.

It is more convenient to carry a picture around for reference than to carry the object that picture represents. It is even more convenient to carry a word, or an idea, in the mind. Man then dispenses with concrete objects and situations as soon as he can. The ideas he has in his mind go with him in a very compact form wherever he goes. Words and ideas require neither space nor transport facilities. Once man has acquired a wealth of ideas or concepts, he can gear up towards new concepts and concepts of a higher order. He then sees, for instance, bottles as belonging to a class of objects called vessels and then vessels as part of a class of objects called utensils, and so on.

The child in the Infant School is dealing with many types of symbols. We provide him with a wealth of real objects and with the opportunity to consolidate his experiences of them, before we expect him to deal with the symbols alone. Ultimately we want him to acquire adult skill in using abstract ideas and symbols, but we know that the quality of his thoughts and the meaning he attaches to symbols depend on full personal acquaintance with the concrete situations behind the abstractions.

The child realises that adults play with these intellectual

toys (words, numbers and signs of all kinds). He wants to know about them and also to be able to play with them. Symbols intrigue him, and he will make every effort to master man's symbols and acquire skill in using them if we give him the chance. If, however, we thrust the symbols upon him too soon, if we try to make him memorise the symbols and tell him what they stand for before the child has a chance to gather his information through experience, then we spoil the child's chance for full understanding, and the symbols may become empty of meaning and difficult for him to handle.

While the child is gathering personal information from his real environment, he is growing familiar with the symbols which permeate an articulate society. He notices that there are numbers on his birthday cards, on the pages of his story book, on the board the school's milkman consults, and on the dinner money he takes to school. There are printed words on packets of paste, on bottles of cough mixture, on notices his teacher makes, in books, on gramophone records and even in the back of a new coat. There are diagrams showing him how to make an experiment, and maps or a globe which tell him about the world. There are note symbols in the song book and paper patterns which show the girls how to cut out a doll's dress. There are pictures and photographs and sometimes films which show him things he has never seen. Always, of course, there are spoken words and they are everywhere all the time.

Some of these symbols are easier than others to recognise. Even so, the child's interpretation of them depends on the concrete experiences he can associate with them. A film tells him more than a photograph about a kangaroo. The photograph tells him more than a picture, but nothing can tell him about the soft feel of the kangaroo's fur better than his own fingers. If we want the child to gain a concept of Africa, we bring him real drums and skins and utensils and put them into his hands before we show him pictures which extend his own impressions.

35

Exploration and language

In spite of the complexity of man's use of symbols, children rarely confuse the various classes of symbols, even before they understand them. They know which symbols represent notes or words, numbers or shapes. Once their interest is aroused and they become aware of the various signs, they seem able to classify them from the start. Symbols are amongst many other of their discoveries. In ordering his world, the child learns to classify symbols as naturally as he learns to classify objects. They are all part of a vast complexity of things he has the urge to explore and ultimately to fit into a pattern.

Of all his symbols, words are the most challenging. Many people think of education in school mainly as a means of instructing the child in his use of words. 'Grammar' schools would seem to be reserved for that purpose. While accepting this as a teacher's most important responsibility, we must not think that we can isolate verbal education. As in all aspects of the child's development, the child will only grow in verbal understanding as a part of his total growth. We know that he needs to explore social relationships, to feel and respond, to move with his hands, his body and his mind, to discover what life is about, what he is and what he is doing here. The effects of education are evident in the whole of his person.

In spite of this we measure the effects of education by the child's verbal skill. Only in special circumstances do we attempt to assess creative ability, mechanical skill, physical competence, or social maturity. Assessment of the personality is often secondary to academic attainment.

The bulk of our children are assessed by examinations which require the children to read, understand and interpret questions and to answer them either on paper or by spoken word. Entrance to a career as an adult is first by paper qualifications which record the result of verbal examinations. Usually a personal interview decides the suitability of a candidate, but it rarely precedes written examination.

We need not quarrel with this procedure if we avoid letting

36

it distort the idea we have of education. The child who has been allowed to develop as fully as possible in every aspect of his person will stand up to being measured in any one of those aspects. We must remember, too, that we are only measuring him in one particular way. We must, in other words, know precisely what examinations assess and whether that is what we want to assess.

Most important of all the teacher must keep examinations in perspective. We don't orientate our work towards them. The child living the full life of the moment ensures his own future. If we want him to become articulate as an adult, we must give him time and opportunity to play with water, to put his finger under the tap, to pour water, splash it, swim in it and drink it, to observe its behaviour in every way possible, before we drill him into recognising drip, dribble, gush, flow and squirt in speech or in print.

We need to remember, too, that significant as words are they are not the only means by which an individual can become articulate. Indeed, many ideas and feelings are more adequately expressed through bodily movement or creative work, and the young learner should have access to symbolism in all its various guises in order to develop really adequate powers of communication. To limit the child's education to a study of words is to limit his powers of development, and his world will only become fully intelligible if he is able to translate the many types of symbols used in representing man's impressions of it. Education in communication involves the exercise of the full range of the child's capacity to experience and respond.

6

Words and thought

Piaget devoted a lifetime to investigating the ways in which children think and reason. He warns us against assuming that because a child seems to learn to talk like adults he has learned to think like them. In examining the child's verbal façade, Piaget shows us how the structuring of the child's thought-processes follows a progression of stages. He emphasises the slow, inward, evolutionary growth of the child's mind as an aspect of the child's total growth.

The development of thought is seen by Piaget and his co-workers as the result of continuous interaction between the child and his environment. The process is twofold. The child endeavours on the one hand to fit information he gains from experience into the developing world within himself, and on the other hand to modify his behaviour so that he fits into the developing world outside himself.

In the early stages these two processes operate side by side. Eventually they fuse and become aspects of the child's mental life. It is through the use of language and in his relationships with other people that the child comes to realise that his is not the only point of view, that all he finds in the world is not only related to him but to other people as well, and that he must give as well as receive and so become part of the great human complex.

38

As these developments take place, the child is also learning how to store his external experiences in the form of thought. Not only can he store his impressions as ideas, he can recall them, relate them and manipulate them. He can reflect, use previous experience in existing circumstances, and even deal with hypothetical situations. This process provides the foundation for intellectual growth.

Piaget was a biologist, and this training may have strongly influenced his point of view, but an observer of children sees much in their behaviour which confirms his findings.[4] His views have certainly helped teachers to understand the many problems associated with the way in which children think and learn. People who live in close contact with children can observe for themselves the way in which a child converts experiences into images he can retain as part of his mental structure, or, in the terms Piaget uses, the way in which he internalises his actions.[5]

Katherine, aged six months, was sitting on the carpet facing a settee. Father was amusing her by playing 'peepo' from behind the settee. After the game had proceeded for a few minutes, whenever father disappeared Katherine waited in suppressed mirth until his head reappeared at the far end of the settee. She *expected* his face to appear because she could recall her impressions of a few moments earlier.

At twelve months, if Katherine were given a spoon she would scramble into her baby-chair. Just holding a spoon in her hand reminded her of what she did with food placed in a bowl on the tray of her chair.

When two-year-old Christopher is tired of walking, he will lift up his arms to his father and say, 'Carry-up!' He has experienced the relief of what happens when father says, 'I'll pick him up and carry him'. Not only can he recall the experience, he is using it to solve his immediate problem.

When three-year-old Susie was given two wrapped toffees by her aunt she put one of them in her pocket, murmuring

39

'Tomorrow'. Susie had reached the stage when she could anticipate a future event.

In the next garden, two four-year-old children were talking. Anita said, 'We're taking a picnic on the arboretum today.'

Vicki enquired, 'How do you know?'

'Well,' explained Anita, 'yesterday Daddy said we would go tomorrow and now tomorrow is today, isn't it?'

Her powers of reasoning were well developed.

In school, as we watch young children learning we observe the internalising process hourly. John, the new arrival finding his way round the school, is shown by his teacher how to identify his classroom door. 'This is my name on the door,' she points out. 'Miss Wetheringham is a long name. Just look for the door with the longest name.' John is five and he cannot read, but he can retain the mental picture of the long patten her name makes and knows his classroom door from all the others which look alike.

Mary is setting the table in the Wendy House. Peter and Win and John are coming for tea. She fetches a handful of plates from the shelf and hopes for the best. When she has set for each person she has a few plates over and puts these back. A week or so later she has devised a more economical procedure. She fetches plates one at a time, one for Peter, one for Win, one for John, and one for Mary. It will be some months perhaps before she can visualise the expected number of places and fetch the appropriate number of plates in one operation.

Derek is making a model steamboat and the funnel must stand up straight. Shaping it from a discarded toilet-roll container is a difficult job. Paste dabbed round the rim at the bottom won't work. He manages eventually to achieve his purpose by using strips of adhesive tape. Derek then makes a second funnel and this time he cuts the bottom like teeth and bends them outwards to provide purchase for his paste.

Sally is experimenting with the balance pans. She has a collection of small objects (dog-biscuits, cotton-bobbins, pegs, beads, etc.) in a biscuit-tin and a box containing twenty one-ounce and other standard weights. She spends a considerable amount of time with the small objects alone, piling things into the pans until she sees the indicator point straight up and down.

She then selects all the little wooden pegs from among her objects. She puts dog-biscuits and cotton-bobbins in one pan and pegs one by one in the other until the two balance. A few days later she takes one of the weights ($\frac{1}{4}$ lb.) and balances the ounce weights against it. She carries on with this experiment using a number of different weights.

Two weeks later a group of children are baking. 'It says half a pound of flour, a quarter of fat . . . ,' one child says, reading out the recipe. Sally goes straight to the weights and selects three. 'This is half a pound, this is a quarter of a pound and that's two ounces,' she says. 'I know because I've tried them.'

Step by step, Sally memorised her actions until eventually they became fused into thought. She could now dispense with early exploratory action and use the idea which had come to represent those actions.

Even as adults we need to go through much the same process when faced with an unfamiliar situation. Learning to drive a car is a concrete learning problem many adults face. We need to handle the gear-box physically before we have a mental impression of our actions when changing gear.

There is obviously a close connection between the activity of thinking and the use of words. As we think we seem to talk to ourselves inwardly. We cannot, however, say that thought and speech are the same thing. Indeed, we often find great difficulty in putting our thoughts into words. Thoughts struggle to take shapes we can recognise and words help us to translate thought into familiar forms.

Often as children explore and experiment they can be heard talking to themselves. This seems to help them in making their discoveries. Putting their actions into words helps them to understand and internalise. Thought can be seen as action stored in the form of words. Sometimes as adults we use verbalising as an aid to action. When we are packing for a holiday, for example, we tell ourselves aloud what to put into the suitcase. When we fit the pieces of a dress pattern over a length of material we argue aloud as to the most advantageous arrangement. Children feel the need to do this more often than adults.

Keith is packing the bricks into their storage box. 'If I put the big ones in first,' he tells himself, 'I can fill the bits at the side with little ones.' . . . 'These two moon shapes fit together and those two squares just go on top of this long one. Miss C said those weren't squares. The sides were squares. They're cubes. And the long one is called an oblong . . .'

If the development of the child's thought-processes is so much a matter of inward growth and maturation, does what we do with him in school make any difference? Will he grow intellectually, irrespective of the environment we provide? Is the enriched life we offer him in school going to help him to develop his ideas sooner or to develop concepts of a higher quality?

Developing concepts sooner will not necessarily mean that the child will be more intelligent or go further in his thinking as an adult. The quality of his ideas is more important than his speed in going through the stages. The quality of his learning depends on the amount of effort the child puts into it. What we *can* do is make the child *want* to learn and this is our first aim when preparing his learning situations in school. The degree of interest for the child in what we offer him will determine the enthusiasm he brings to the job. This is the secret of good teaching: to stimulate the desire to be taught. We realise, too, that a wide range of situations to explore will add meaning to the words and ideas the child acquires. Words full of meaning provide enriched material for the stuff of his thoughts. These thoughts are a synthesis of the child's inward experiences and of the experiences he finds in his outer world.

The child's understanding of both himself and the world grows as an aspect of his total development. As he acquires an ever-widening vocabulary of words to represent his stored experiences his mental powers mature and he becomes increasingly more capable of using symbolic processes. The child alone can make the effort to acquire the skill of thought and understanding. All we can do is provide him with first-class opportunities and then allow him all the time he needs.

7

Words and personality

We no longer believe that a child inherits his personality. He may inherit certain temperamental and physical characteristics, and intelligence has much to do with innate ability, but the way in which this basic material will develop into the child's personal pattern depends on how and what he learns. As he grows older he may resemble his father or mother because he has used them as a pattern on which to model himself. He has become like them by imitating their behaviour and adopting their attitudes. He depends on them almost entirely during his most formative years, and they play a leading role in the development of his individual personal pattern.

Language in its many forms provides the link between the child and other people. Through communicating with others the child finds out about other people and about himself, but before he can do this he must become aware of himself as a separate person.

During his first months the baby moves his limbs and body about. He explores the shape of himself with his hands and finds out where he stops and the world outside himself begins. As he becomes more aware of his separate existence and realises that he is a different person from the mother who feeds him and cares for him, the approval or disapproval of that other person helps him to learn what sort of a person he is.

44

He wants to please the person he depends on, if only to secure the satisfaction of his needs. He knows from mother's reactions which of the things he is pleases her (the 'Yes' things) and which do not (the 'No' things).

Even though he doesn't understand mother's words at this early stage, the child knows the difference between 'Good boy' and 'Naughty boy', if only by the tone of her voice and the emotional message he receives from her. Once he has acquired words for himself, learning about self goes ahead quickly. He finds that, in his turn, he can register approval or disapproval of others, to which they respond. Most parents have experienced their child's discovery and delight in the power of 'No'.

The fact that he can manipulate others and make them respond to him helps the child to become increasingly aware of himself. He is then in a position to get to know that self. The first two years of his life are an extremely important period of personal development. We know from the evidence of deaf children, whose language is impaired, how handicapped they are without the use of words.[6]

Normally a child of two will know his own name. He can label himself and he alone bears that particular label. He can use his name to refer to himself and others understand. When Kathie, aged two years and one month, had finished her pudding she would say, 'Good Kaffie'. If she were reprimanded she would murmur, 'Kaffie gone'. By the time she was three she had developed much further her powers of self-identification. One day she was trying to sweep the yard with an enormous brush and father came to her rescue. Kathie clung determinedly to the brush and scowled. 'Do it afelf,' she asserted.

Some children even on entering school are unable to apply the pronoun words to themselves. Although they are well able to say 'me, mine', etc., and will even understand what the adult means when he refers to 'your so-and-so', they get very

45

confused when it comes to using these substitutes for their own name. Tony, aged five and a half, tried to reason this out.

'You said that it [a tidy box] was "yours" and that means it's Tony's.' His teacher nodded: 'When you talk about that box you say, "It is mine" or "my box".' To which Tony replied, 'So yours is the same as mine.' A week later the penny had dropped and Tony took great delight in labelling all that was 'mine'.

The development of the child's self-idea is a twofold process. He finds out, on the one hand, what idea other people have of him by what they say to him and about him. At the same time he discovers what he is like through experiences such as using materials which provide him with adequate opportunity for self-expression. The child sees in his own work and in the finished product something of himself. Likewise, when he tries to use father's hammer or to run like big brother, more of himself is revealed.

By the time he is two the child has established at least an awareness of the bodily self. With the aid now of language, he can label himself 'Billy'. He can now understand that when people use his name, 'Billy is a good boy', 'Billy has ten little toes', 'This is for Billy', they see him as a separate entity. When they use his name he can attach the things they say to himself. His name identifies and it remains extremely significant to him for the rest of his life.

It is important for the child to develop a favourable but authentic idea of himself and his abilities. He must learn to accept and like himself before he can learn to accept and like others. On the other hand he must know his limitations, for if his levels of attainment are set too high he will feel a failure and be unable to adjust to life as it is.

The idea of what he is as a physical person provides the anchorage for his psychological self. First his parents and family and then friends of the family will tell him what he is like. 'Billy is tall for his age.' 'You've got a bonny boy there' (to his mother). 'Billy's going to be a proper little tear-about.' 'You're going to be a wow with the girls, Billy. Just like your father.' The mirror confirms this message and Billy gains respect for this bodily self which is to serve him for the whole of his life.

Not all children, of course, gain a favourable impression of self. 'Just look at the ugly little brat! Screaming his head off, he is!' 'You get those bandy legs from your Uncle Tom, Jimmy. None of your mother's side are like that.' The handicapped child particularly needs very special help.

Ideas of bodily self are interwoven with self-ideas which are not only physical. The 'good boy' refers to something inside the bodily self. 'He's a clever little lad, he is.' 'Our Billy's forward for his age. Perhaps he'll get to the high school.' 'Give Judy one of your sweeties, Billy. Be kind to her when she comes to play with you.' 'Billy's such a happy child!'

At the same time Billy is trying to explore other selves, often by imitating what interests him in other people. He pretends to be mother and wants a basket to pop things in at the supermarket. He gets under the table and barks like a dog. He puffs around the station platform and his curiosity is so intense that he becomes that train for the time being. In this way he discovers that things have no selves, but that people have selves and that he can graft parts of those selves on to his own.[7]

When the child comes into school his opportunities are widened. This may be the first time he has encountered at close quarters children of his own age. They will soon prove to him that life isn't centred in his feelings and needs, that he will have to develop as deep an awareness of others as he has of himself. Teachers and other adults in the school will further confirm his realistic view of himself and help him to adjust his own demands so that he can fit in with others. By this time much of his exchange with other people takes place in the form of words.

Jeremy started school on his fifth birthday. He brought a

47

handful of birthday cards and his new tractor. His teacher welcomed him. 'Hello! You're Jeremy, aren't you? You look a big sensible boy, and I'm going to give you a special job. We have two lots of birthday cards today. Would you like to stand them up on this table and then we'll show them to the other boys and girls.'

Feeling important, Jeremy forgot his initial apprehension. He put his tractor on the floor and set to work on the cards. Peter, an established member of the group, admired the tractor. 'How does it tip up?' He crouched down to investigate.

Jeremy paused, torn between his desire to complete his important job and his urge to protect his tractor. He went on with his job and kept a vigilant eye on Peter's investigations. Peter fumbled. 'Don't think it works,' he muttered in disgust.

'Does!' Jeremy hastened to demonstrate. 'If we'd got some soil I'd show you.' Peter pointed through the classroom window. 'There's soil out there,' he said. 'We can go out when it isn't raining.' Jeremy assumed the role of leadership. 'I'll show you,' he offered. 'And you can help.' Fresh aspects of his personality were opening up.

Through these early years the child explores any materials which come his way. With effort and patience he discovers that he has power over materials, he can find out what they will do, and then he can make them serve his purpose. As a result of his manipulation there is often an end-product and this provides visible evidence of what he can do and what he is like. His end-product differs from the end-product of others. It is as unique to him as his personality is.

Mother gave June, aged three, a piece of pastry dough to keep her busy until the baking was finished. Jane kneaded, rolled and shaped it, and her finished biscuits went into the oven. Her biscuits were clearly different from Mother's. Auntie, coming into the kitchen, said, 'Are these Jane's biscuits? I'll have one of these. They're a funny shape but they're scrumptious You're going to be a good cook, Jane.'

When Jane came into school she spent hours handling clay. Even after she had made her initial discoveries she was contented to knead it and pummel it, making a shape and then squeezing it out of existence. One day she sat in front of her lump of clay completely absorbed, watching it shape under her fingers.

'I'm going to make a man,' she murmured. 'I'll squeeze out this piece for his head . . . Now he must have some arms . . . and some legs . . .' She talked as she worked and eventually sat back.

'I've made you,' she smiled at her clay man. 'I must give you a name because you're a real man. You're Bumps.' In her role of creator she had implanted a grain of herself in what she created and therefore she loved it. Having created it, she named it and so confirmed its existence.

In the crude creative work of our children we see much of what they are as people. Listening to the child's creative use of words, in the form of speech, provides us with the best clue to the child's personality. Later he will also learn to put these things on paper.

Anne was happily absorbed in painting. 'I'm going to paint my house blue, because it's quiet like the sky. When I'm big I'll have a room with a blue carpet and blue paper on the wall. It'll be pretty and smell nice and nobody will shout.' It was easy for the teacher who observed this activity to catch a glimpse of Anne as an adult. In a few words Anne revealed the idea of herself which would influence her development towards adult personality.

As adults we may learn much about another person from his appearance and from the way he behaves, but it is often in conversation that we reach through to his innermost thoughts. Words play an important part in the development of a personality pattern, and the way in which a man uses his words is highly indicative of his personality.

8

Playing with symbols

By symbols we mean emblems which represent something else. Man's use of symbols depends on common agreement as to the meaning of the emblems he uses.

The idea of letting one thing stand for another develops at a very early stage and we can watch in children their progression towards the use of symbols. Jeremy at eighteen months was turning the pages of a picture book with his father. A large golden pear on one page attracted his attention. He pretended to pick it from the page and put it into his mouth. He then went through the book, repeating the procedure with other pictures of fruit. He knew that the picture stood for the real object.

Janet's favourite game at the age of four was playing at tea-parties. She needed few properties and would use stones or leaves for plates, food, even people. Sometimes she dispensed with real objects altogether and would use action alone in place of them.

At a very early age a child likes to make a mark on paper. By the time he is three he can use many kinds of media and will scribble with pencil and charcoal or paint and crayon. The three-year-old will try in his two-dimensional pictures to represent things he has seen. By making two-dimensional pictures represent his impression of three-dimensional objects he performs a considerable feat. A study of children's scribble reveals some interesting features. There is a strong resemblance in the symbol for a man whichever human race the child belongs to. There would seem to be a sequence of stages, too, in the development of the picture from the ball-and-stick man of the three-year-old to the detailed figure in profile of the nine-year-old child.

Amongst these early scribblings the child will include letters and numbers, road-signs and notes. The seven-year-old may even try to draw a diagrammatic view of a street or perhaps a 'map of my way to the seaside'. Sometimes a child will know what his symbols stand for. Sometimes he will tell the onlooker incorrectly what they are supposed to represent. Sometimes he will ask, 'What does this say?'

Understanding of different types of symbols does not come to the child in any particular order. He doesn't necessarily learn to recognise words before maps or numbers before notes. As the child's thought-processes become more definitely structured and his capacity for dealing with the abstract develops, the idea of man's use of symbols grows on him.

Right from his early recognition of symbols the child begins to discriminate between the kinds of symbols which represent words, numbers, notes, road-signs, songs. He never tries to represent a song by using numbers. As his powers of discrimination develop he begins to recognise the differences between symbols of the same type, as between word patterns for example. If we urge him too soon to discriminate between word patterns, he starts to become confused, loses confidence and may even grow to fear the very symbols which have been his toys until the adult spoiled his game. His natural curiosity is very great. Once he is familiar with his symbols, he is extremely anxious to interpret them. He delights in his discoveries. Why, in our anxiety, do we tend to rush him and turn his joy into apprehension, and then blame him because he flounders?

The child's world is permeated by these symbols and he

meets them hourly as a part of everything he is doing. He associates them with his emotional and physical state at the time of contact. Amidst the excitement of going on holiday he meets the symbol which stands for the road on Daddy's map. He knows the symbol on the clock which indicates dinnertime, the number on his card which says he is five, the notes which stand for 'Happy Birthday to You'. He can discriminate between 'Push' and 'Pull' on the swing doors. He knows what arrows mean and the road-sign which says 'No Entry'.

These symbols the child meets are just as exciting as any other of his discoveries. He enjoys playing with them and speculating about their meaning. He is free to interpret them as he decides and the meaning he attaches at this stage is his personal decision. These symbols will remain his friends until the adult starts to isolate them from the pleasurable experiences the child associates with them, and so to divorce them of meaning. It is the adult who reduces the child's handling of symbols to a form of drill or even of drudgery.

The child's interest in symbols is a natural stage in his growing concept of his world. In his own good time he will need the help of the adult to interpret them precisely and use them with skill. Adults often fail him by their lack of confidence in his natural aptitude for development. They can create in the child positive distaste for symbols and a lack of confidence in dealing with them.

Amongst the many symbols employed by a literate society, numbers play a highly important role. They represent the ordering of the universe. Again the young child performs a tremendous feat in reducing his experiences to mathematical order.

Mary loved playing with mother's button-box. At the age of four she would gather together those which were similar in some way. She was probably unaware that they had any particular quality in common; they simply seemed to go together. A few weeks later she approached the activity with a particular criterion in mind. 'I'll have all the red ones here . . . all the blue ones . . . the big ones . . . the small ones . . . the big blue . . . the little red . . .', and, later still, even such refinements as 'the big blue with two holes' and so on.

In school children manipulate much of their material in this way. All the empty milk bottles are assigned to one end of the milk crate. Bricks are sorted according to size or shape or purpose. At a certain stage number becomes a significant quality of groups. Many groups have the quality of five, or three, or two. From all such similar groups the idea of five, or three, or two is extracted. The idea then stands for all groups containing that number of objects.

The child is now ready to understand the sound of the word 'five'. It is at a later stage that the printed symbol 5 is recognised as standing for his experiences of five. The symbol 5 is a precise and economical way of representing all he understands from these experiences. He does not necessarily know yet that five comes after four and before six, or that the five group is the four group with one added. He may be quite unaware that the adult has decided on a particular order for naming the symbols in sequence, 'One, two, three, four, five'. It may not be until he is six or seven that he is ready to count with any idea of what his counting means.

Yet how often do we find the fond parent presenting her five-year-old son to a teacher with the assurance that 'He can count. Show teacher how you can count, Barry. One, two, three . . .' Sometimes, even teachers fall into the trap of believing that because the child is able to say and repeat these words he knows what counting means. He must know about groups and their names before he can put them in order and so see the relationship between them. In *Discovering the Physical World* we consider in greater detail the development of mathematical ideas and the use of mathematical symbols.

When talking to children and listening to what they say,

we realise that they have acquired a great many terms and expressions before they come into school and that the meaning they attach to these terms is shallow and imprecise. One of the teacher's main responsibilities is to help the child to enlarge the meaning of the terms he uses and to use them more precisely. The most effective way of doing this is to provide extensive experiences and to encourage the child to talk about these experiences.

A group of objects had been set out for the children to handle. One little girl picked up a glass paper-weight and admired it. 'It's soft,' she said appreciatively. This was an opportunity for the teacher to give her the word 'smooth' and at the same time let the child handle and describe a number of objects which were either soft or smooth. Later she found objects such as fur and silk, which were both soft and smooth.

David was trying to find a piece of wood which he and Ian could shape into an oar for their boat. He held a length in his hand. 'This one won't do,' he explained. 'I want a piece that's a bit less long.' Because he knew 'short' when he spoke about his friend being a 'short boy', it came as quite a surprise to his teacher that he didn't know 'shorter', and he seemed even more doubtful about applying this term to a piece of wood.

Terry used the word 'millions' as often as he could. Saying it obviously gave him great satisfaction. He sensed it was important in some way and no doubt he connected it with affluence. 'Go on, have a toffee, Miss. I've got millions.' 'There was a fire last night in our street and the fire-engines came. There were millions and millions of firemen . . .' He also used it in more unusual ways. 'Our Jean can stand up now, but I'm millions bigger than she is . . .' Not only did Terry need help with the meaning of words which were familiar to him, he needed to add equally exciting words to his vocabulary.

When children are stimulated to talk and then encouraged to do so freely, we are able to assess the quality of the words they use. If adults drown children in words and give them little opportunity to use words themselves, children will acquire a vocabulary with little conceptual foundation. The modern classroom is full of the sound of children's chatter, of children's questions, and of children thinking aloud. In such classrooms children are having every chance to become articulate adults with well-furnished minds.

9

The child's speech

Listening to speech is fascinating, for speech is eloquent of personality. Even when the words used are indecipherable, the tone of a speaker's voice and the way in which he uses speech reveals much of his background. An imaginative listener can set the speaker in his home, envisage situations he is likely to encounter, and prognosticate about his reactions. When words are audible, even more is revealed. At every age a person is judged by his speech, and speech is highly expressive of the person.

A child learns to speak between the time of his birth and the age of two. The main part of the job has been done before he comes into school.[8] Speech demands of the child not only the ability to vocalise and use words which mean something to him and to others, but also the necessity to put words together to form patterns which are socially acceptable. In speech, words are used as bricks and are carefully structured into artistic forms of communication.

Some of our children have acquired good speech forms before they enter school. Others will remain inarticulate through many of their primary years. The more inarticulate the child is, the greater is his need for expert help from an articulate adult. Unfortunately many of our inarticulate children attend schools where the adult/child ratio is least favourable. The articulate parent often manages to place his child in a small class where talk between teacher and child is assured, but children of less favoured parents do not have such regular opportunities and so their first educational need is often skimped.

Many children are eager to use the speech they have when they come into school, and they will chatter incessantly if given the chance. Speech practice is as normal to them as breathing and moving. In a few cases the teacher's problem is in getting children to speak; more often her problem is in helping them to speak effectively and with greater purpose.

Although teachers have always recognised the need for the child to practise his speech, it is only in recent years that the utmost need for that practice to be spontaneous has been recognised. Formal provision for speech in the form of object lessons, conversation, and verbal news periods are giving way to free interchange between child and child and between child and adult. It is not natural for young children to remain still and silent for long periods. The control of the class teacher is no longer judged by her ability to keep the children just where she wants them and silent until spoken to. She holds the reins by guiding the children through their spontaneous chatter towards becoming articulate. The harmonious hum of a happy workshop suggests a control within which the child's individual modes of expression can flourish.

The spontaneous speech of the child is stimulated in a variety of situations. It provides him with a means of getting to know other children. The content is not nearly so important as the act of exchanging words, so that speech forms a bridge between two people. If some situation such as mealtime provides a common interest, so much the better. Quite often, however, the speech of young children consists of a series of statements rather than conversation. Anita and Dave, both aged five, were sitting next to one another at the dinner table. They were eating creamed rice.

Anita: 'My spoon's little.'

Dave: 'Creamed rice is best.'

Anita: 'I can't get very much with a little spoon.'

Dave: 'I can eat lots and lots of creamed rice.'

Anita: 'The spoon in the dish is better. I'm using that.'

Two children may share an activity and appear to be exchanging their views. A careful listener will discover that their exchanges have little to do with the activity they share. Jimmy and Ron, aged seven, were constructing a lighthouse. Their problem appeared to be how to make the light-holder stay in place. Their fingers exchanged suggestions about strips of tape and various adhesives. What they were actually talking about was the football match they had witnessed with their respective fathers on the previous Saturday.

A highly educative use of speech is that which arises from the need to tell someone about an exciting experience. School offers the child particularly good opportunities in this direction. Each morning children burst into the classroom, scarcely able to wait to pour out their experiences to the teacher, who listens with more patience than parents often have time for. They have here the chance also to tell a whole group of listeners. School is full of exciting things to do and speech is a ready vehicle for expressing personal reactions to these experiences. The skilful teacher uses this expressive form of speech as the material for creative writing and reading (see Chapter 18).

When life is exciting and full of curious things, questions arise in the mind of a child. Here again school is very well equipped with mature adult minds and informative books. The questions from children pour freely and teachers recognise in them highly effective opportunities for learning. The questions the child asks spontaneously are far more important than those asked by the teacher. They do, in fact, indicate the quality of provision made in the environment. If the teacher's material is sound and appropriate, it will provoke questions which lead to learning that is vital and relevant to the individual child.

Verbal reasoning is also often evident in the spontaneous speech of the child. Peter, aged six, crouching on the pavement, peered intently at the cracks between the flagstones. 'They're going in and out and there's millions of them. They're ants. My Dad said they're ants. There must be lots of them down there. They make tunnels, like on TV. It must be all tunnels with ants rushing up and down under here. Perhaps they talk like people, not like ants. When they make tunnels, or they want to know which way to go, they must talk. I don't want to be an ant and live under there with people walking on top of me . . .'

Sometimes when children talk to themselves they are thinking aloud. Sometimes they are talking for the sheer delight of hearing the words. A small boy paraded the bank, while his father cashed a cheque, murmuring, 'The Dukes of Hamilton and Porchester . . . The Dukes of Hamilton and Porchester . . . The Dukes of Hamilton and . . .'

The teacher, then, has little difficulty in encouraging the normal child to practise speech.[9] The average four- to five-year-old will say approximately 2,000 words per day. The teacher has an important part to play both in what the child talks about and how he says it. The articulate person has something of interest to say and is able to say it so that he is understood. However capable of saying words a child is, his speech is of little interest either to himself or to others unless it is founded on a wealth of interesting things that he can do. Teachers and parents are responsible for furnishing the young child's mind, so that the ideas behind his words are rich and vivid. What the child thinks and talks about depends on what he sees and feels and hears. This is the fundamental reason behind the present-day classroom, alive with objects calculated to stimulate and extend curiosity and excite interest. Sometimes the uninitiated onlooker finds it difficult to link the

59

child's play amongst these objects with learning which takes place in the mind, but it is in his concrete surroundings that the contents of a child's mind first form.

During the first years in school children need a great deal of help with their modes of speech. We are more concerned with helping the child to make himself understood and with the quality of voice he uses than in instilling rules for grammatical speech. Correct speech is very much a matter of taste and fashion. 'Speech is how people speak, not how some authority thinks they ought to speak' (Plowden, para. 611). A person could memorise all the rules of grammar and still be inarticulate.

A child will convey his meaning if he understands what he is talking about and if his pronunciation is clear and accurate. Many of our children suffer from slovenly speech or from imitating poor speech patterns. The best possible help a teacher can give is the good, clear, natural example of her own speech and the encouragement to express ideas as precisely as possible. 'You know. It was a thingumy' does not describe the insect Jane found under the stones on the garden path. With help from her teacher she can do better.

Teachers have for many years sensed the usefulness of drama as an aid to good speech and mastery of the mother tongue. We have seen how the speech of the very young child is associated with his movements. The baby's 'ma-ma' sound, the babbling of the baby enjoying the satisfaction of waving his arms and legs about, the squeals, shouts and words which accompany early crawling, running, eating and dressing are evidence of the link between doing and speech.

As the child grows older he will think aloud as he plays. Ian, aged three and a half, playing with his wooden engine, accompanied each action with words. 'I'm going to put some coal in here and then you'll steam . . . Now we're ready and we're going a long way to London . . .' This association of words and movement is quite natural to the child, and in drama we see the synthesis of speech, gesture and movement.

Formal drama has no place in the Infant School. A repetition of prescribed actions, accompanied by words which are put into the mouth of the child, do little for him either linguistically or emotionally. The free dramatic play of the child is a very different matter. A child is often liberated in his speech through his own make-believe. His passive vocabulary becomes active as his thoughts and feelings take the shape of words.

Simple equipment in the Wendy House, a few drapes and simple properties, will fire the child's imagination. He will *become* his mother or father, the policeman, the school inspector, the astronaut, or the teacher. His imagination creates the scene and his mind finds words to clothe his imagination. In his free dramatic play we see the preliminary practice of speech which precedes reading, writing, reasoning and understanding. At the same time the child is learning to put himself into the shoes of another person, which helps his speech to develop from the egocentric speech of babyhood into the socialised speech of the adult.

Time spent in helping the child to develop his powers of speech will provide us with an excellent means of discovering and liberating the child's personality.

10

Words in use

In school words are used in many ways. They are used, mainly by the teacher, for instruction. They are used for asking questions and providing answers. They are used as a means of expressing oneself, often with the hope of conveying meaning but sometimes as a form of verbal gesture as in 'Bother!', 'Good!', 'Oo!', 'Ah!', 'Oh dear!' They are frequently used to report, record and describe. Sometimes they are used purely for pleasure.

Where the education of the young child is concerned, the emphasis is on the spoken uses of words. As the child matures, the many uses of words on paper play an equally important role. Even in higher and further education, we try to keep a balance between the spoken and the written word in its various forms.

At one time it was the teacher who did most of the talking and much of what she said took the form of instruction and questions. Changing ideas as to her role and the relative function of instruction in the learning situation have resulted in a change in emphasis. Today, it is the child who is encouraged to do most of the talking and it is more often he who asks the questions.

On entering school the child is perhaps more used to instruction as a speech form used by older people towards him than any other form. During his early days in school the child expects the teacher to initiate speech between them and a few simple instructions on her part help to make him feel at home. The teacher tells the child what to do with his coat, which tidy box he can regard as his own, where he can find a rubber apron, and so on. She conveys to him the stability and ordering of his new workshop. She shows him where he fits into it and gives him the feeling that he belongs. She will soon know by the way he interprets her instructions something about his intellect and personality.

Once a child has learned how to frame questions, he has the most effective means of assuaging his insatiable curiosity. If school provides an interesting environment, children will ask endless questions to extend or confirm their discoveries. The teacher's job is not always to provide an immediate answer. The spirit of enquiry can be maintained by providing further material which will lead the child towards finding his own answers. While helping the child to find answers from books or to explore further, the teacher keeps the situation alive. Answers given too readily are limiting and may terminate thought by terminating curiosity and enquiry. The teacher's answer sometimes takes the form of another question.

While the bulk of the child's questions are about things and facts, some are about life and living together. These are questions he cannot answer through further exploration of objects and materials. They are the most difficult questions of all for the adult to answer, for in answering we have no body of knowledge to refer to, but depend on personal opinion, which is emotionally biased.

When a child asks a question we know that he already understands something of the nature of the problem, for otherwise he wouldn't know what to ask. When Derek asks, 'Are you nearly dead now you're old, Grandma?', he has recognised the connection between age and death. It's no use trying to evade the question by telling him not to be rude or that he isn't old

63

enough to understand. He needs a simple and sincere reply, otherwise old age may seem to hold something sinister. On the other hand he does not need a long and involved analysis of the relationship between old age and death. His precise question should be answered as accurately and concisely as possible and at his own level of understanding. Sometimes by turning the question back on the child we discover how much he understands. A question may sound profound when in fact it is quite elementary. The enquiry, 'What will happen to pussy now she's dead?' may require the answer, 'We shall bury her', rather than involved explanations of pussy's chance of eternity.

A child may ask such a question at intervals as he matures. Each occasion represents a stage in his understanding and he can progress in this way towards full knowledge.

The visitor to the Infant School is invariably asked, 'Who are you?', or 'Are you the inspector?' or 'What is your name?' The child needs to identify, by naming the unfamiliar. This is particularly important when the unknown is a person. By naming the person, fear of that person is removed. The child will need to know, too, 'Where do you come from?', 'Have you a husband?', et cetera. The new person has to be fitted into the child's plan of his world. This is part of his attempt to reduce his environment to something he can understand.

As the child learns to master his mother tongue, he finds in words a medium through which he can express what he feels and thinks. Being able to express what he feels helps him to understand and come to terms with his feelings. It is also a means of conveying his feelings to others. The use of speech may come to replace aggressive action. Once a child can tell his teacher that he 'wants a tractor like John's, but he can't because his Mum's got no money', he doesn't need to snatch John's tractor as he plays with it and try to smash it up. Talking about his feelings instead of showing them in action applies to positive as well as negative emotions. The child who

64

can tell his teacher he likes her will soon resist the temptation to fling his arms round her skirt every time he sees her. His social behaviour matures as he acquires the ability to convey his impressions to others.

The child's expressive use of words is fostered in school. We give him much to talk about, to provoke feeling. We then help him to translate his experiences into words in such a way that they are understood and shared by other people. The child's recording takes a number of forms, such as picture-making, modelling, drama and movement. Recording in words is at first wholly in the form of speech. Only when the child is fully articulate do we expect him to record on paper. There is no purpose at all in the child copying what the teacher has written until he is able to tell her what to write down. We shall not speed the process of writing creatively by expecting the child to copy words representing ideas and expressions which originated in the mind of another person. Too often children are turned against record-making because they are expected to record on paper with words when verbal recording is as much as they can manage.

Two boys were experimenting with water. With the aid of a nail and a hammer they pierced holes in the base of equal-sized tins, one hole in the first tin and two in the second. They filled both tins with water and counted slowly as they emptied. One tin emptied on the twenty-ninth count, the second ran on until they had counted fifty-five. They described the situation as: 'If the tin has two holes, it empties in twenty-nine, but if it has only one hole, it takes fifty-five.' Their teacher, overhearing this, suggested: 'You can write about your experiment in our Discovery Book. I'll help you to say it properly.' She spent ten patient minutes with the two boys, bending their description to an acceptable form which she wrote down for them to copy. They struggled for the rest of the morning and eventually earned the approval of their teacher. They avoided the water experiments for the rest of the week.

In another situation, a boy and a girl were making similar experiments. This time holes were pierced down the sides of a tin. There was great excitement when the tin was filled and allowed to empty. 'It spurts right out. It's more at the bottom. When the tins get nearly empty the spurts get little.' Their teacher joined them in their discussion. 'What happened?' She encouraged them to describe in greater detail, helping them here and there with a more appropriate word and introducing the term 'jet'. She then reminded them of an earlier experiment. 'Do you remember how you syphoned water out of the bucket? You could syphon water from this bucket into the tin and keep it full for quite a long time.' Their experiments continued and their vocabulary increased to include the terms 'water pressure' and 'adjust'. Verbal recording was far more appropriate than written or even pictorial recording at this stage.

The child's earliest utterances are a pleasure to him. The baby babbles for the sheer delight of hearing himself and for the rhythmic satisfaction babbling brings him. At all stages feeling permeates the child's use of words. Repetition adds a sense of security to this pleasure. Many nursery rhymes and jingles owe their popularity to the child's instinctive love of sound and rhythm. 'Pat-a-cake, pat-a-cake . . .' is a favourite in most homes. (The child's rhythmic use of words is explored more fully in *Senses and Sensitivity* in this series.)

This love and delight in the use of words should be retained throughout life. It is far more important to enjoy one's mother tongue than to memorise patterns of printed words or to obey all the rules of grammar. A child of six will acquire words such as hippopotamus, elephant, supersonic, transfusion, evaporation, simply because he enjoys the rhythmic sound of them. They have magic and he will master them when words like to, at, in, bad, sad leave him unmoved.

Mastery of words makes them the child's playthings, and the seven- to eight-year-old will revel in puns and riddles,

66

nonsense rhymes and jingles, secret codes and name calling, slang and foreign words, swearing and forbidden words. He will also appreciate the poetic use of words.

By the time the child leaves the Infant School he should be handling words with confidence and know enough about them to be able to play with them and use them imaginatively. This playing with words is the exploratory aspect of his learning about them. He must be given time to accomplish this exploratory stage thoroughly before hastening on to formal uses of words. Words need never become a worry to the child, and the adults in the child's life are responsible for sustaining his delight in them.

11

The importance of literacy

Man is justifiably proud of his ability to use words. He alone uses language. While all but the simplest animals have developed elementary forms of communication, only man employs conventionalised gestures and sounds. From time to time we come across some higher form of animal life, such as the chimpanzee, the dog, or even the parrot, which has been taught by man to 'say' words. These words signify little to the animal and cannot be used by it to communicate with a fellow animal. Only man uses sounds and gestures which convey a verbal message. Only man, by walking upright, has liberated his hands and so can use language in written form.

Man's words, then, mark him off from other forms of life. Through his use of words he can rise to abstract thought and so can live at levels quite unknown to animals. It follows naturally that man's verbal accomplishment is a measure of his capacity to make successful adjustments to his world.

'Personal and social adequacy depend on being articulate, on having the words and language structures with which to think, to communicate what is thought and to understand what is heard or read' (Newsom Report).[10]

One of our main functions as a teacher or parent is to help the child to build up a varied and meaningful vocabulary and to help him to use his words with skill and artistry. When we are

68

dealing with the young child we realise that his words are very intimately woven into his personal growth and that he is not yet ready to separate out his study of words from other aspects of his learning. His language is a pattern of habits rooted deeply in his personality, and what the child does with language in school needs to be built into his total language pattern.

As we have seen, in our society the child's environment is permeated by language. Everything he does demands of him that he shall use language. He meets his words embodied in all his experiences. When we try to help him to develop the use of his words we need to remember that they are part of what he is doing, a link in a sequence of activities and not something he can deal with in isolation. The philosopher may be able to contemplate the significance of the word 'good', but the child will only understand it in connection with himself or things he likes.

Our ultimate aim for the child is that he shall be able to initiate communication by expressing himself in spoken and written speech, that he shall be able to complete the communication by understanding the spoken and written speech of others, and that he shall love and enjoy words, and appreciate the appeal of literature.

In Western cultures a very high value is set on reading ability. Much of what the child learns in school depends on his ability to deal with printed words. In some societies a child would be taught to protect himself and hunt heads as an introduction to adult life. In our country teachers and parents see reading as the key to learning. Sometimes, indeed, they seem to become obsessed by the business of teaching the child to read.

In the fifteenth century the invention in Europe of printing by movable type revolutionised the reproduction of literary matter. This event is responsible for the importance of print in our lives today, and the behaviour of teachers and children in school is profoundly affected by the printed word. On occasions we even lose sight of what printed words stand for;

they seem to assume intrinsic value and dominate the purpose and life of the school. When this happens the joyful discovery of words turns to drudgery, and we have only ourselves to blame if the results are disappointing.

Because of man's recognition of the importance and power of words, intellectual capacity and educational performance are assessed through linguistic skill. The child whose speech is poor and whose understanding of words is shallow finds the recognition of words in print a very great problem, and much of what he is expected to do in the way of learning in school is barred to him. As he proceeds to the Junior School he finds he can make little use of what school offers. His intellectual rating becomes progressively lower than it should be.

Tests of intelligence are verbally based. They take the form of spoken or printed questions and problems which require verbal responses. Even the non-verbal type of intelligence test depends considerably on the child's ability to reason by talking to himself or by using words internally.

These pressures have had a disastrous effect on the life of the schools. Linguistic accomplishment has become an end in itself rather than the natural product of experience. Once this happens, the use of words in a particular way, as in the case of reading cr writing, gets out of perspective. Some teachers and parents are satisfied if a child can articulate words from a printed book and make the shape of them accurately on paper. The true purpose and use of words become lost in the empty pursuit of such limited skills, and the effects of education are assessed more and more exclusively by verbal examination.

Few topics of discussion create a more emotional response amongst literate adults than the teaching of reading. No doubt many adults today learned to associate their early reading stages with emotional situations, not all of which were very pleasant. We must avoid imposing on our children the dreary and disturbing experiences we were exposed to as children.

Many people firmly believe that the Infant School should turn out accomplished readers, forgetting that learning to read is a prolonged and slow development which need not worry any child who has learned to speak and who is physically equipped to discriminate between visual patterns. The actual recognition of printed words is part of a process which started at birth and will continue until the day of death. At each stage in the child's school life he needs help with the reading process. Students entering college often find they need a great deal of help when they are faced with unfamiliar material and unexpected extensions to their vocabulary. The unfortunate idea that reading happens once and for all in the Infant School has created a great deal of misunderstanding about the school's true function. Teachers under unnatural pressure are filled with anxiety which conveys itself to their pupils.

From time to time depressing reports about the standard of reading in this country appear in the Press. These reports seem to receive more attention than investigations undertaken by the Department of Education between 1948 and 1964 which make it clear that the standard as a whole has been going up steadily since the war. Some research workers seem to delight in discovering and exposing poor reading skill, and this kind of publicity can have a very detrimental effect on the teachers of young children. It takes confidence and conviction to resist these pressures and protect the right of children to develop not only in verbal skill but in all aspects of their personalities.

Junior and Secondary Schools must understand the part they play in the reading process. Many children need help all the way and most need help at some time or other, even after they have grown up. The help of a friend with an Income Tax form is frequently sought by quite intelligent adults. Learning to read is not a feat accomplished once and for all time. It is not a circus trick or a status symbol. It is part of the total development of the child's understanding of a literate society. When we recognise this fully, we shall be in a position

71

to deal with the job of helping the child to accomplish his reading far more effectively than we do at present. If we have faith in the child's ability to learn to speak, why can't we extend some of that faith to his ability to grow into the use of the visible extension of speech—the printed word? It is lack of faith on the part of the adult which creates some of the problems associated with learning to read. A child beset by anxious parents and teachers, who make words a nightmare for him, is not likely to read with ease and delight. If he is ultimately condemned as being dull, whose is the fault?

12

The child's home background

The child learns to speak in his home, and his family will play an important part in the development of his language for the greater part of his childhood. As the child's circle of acquaintances and experiences widens, many influences will impinge on his speech. The confidence of success or the anxiety of a difficult job or the warmth of feeling excited by a romantic relationship will add qualities to his voice and words to his vocabulary. A fresh human situation, such as a university education or the dialect used by workmates in an unfamiliar town, can influence his speech forcefully. He may even acquire a veneer of speech in contrast to his native tongue, but the underlying structure of his speech will remain and may even take him by surprise in a relaxed moment. The speech a person learns during his early, highly impressionable years will remain the foundation of his speaking for the rest of his life. The quality of the child's early linguistic environment will remain the most important factor affecting his linguistic development.

Children from different backgrounds have different opportunities for learning speech and this affects later learning. Interest in the study of social class differences in language and thought has intensified in recent years as a result of the work of investigators such as Bernstein with English children and Jensen with American children.[11] Their findings suggest that

73

underprivileged children are most severely handicapped by poor speech and underdeveloped thought-processes. In our educational system, which is primarily designed to cater for middle-class children, the children from underprivileged homes fail dismally and possible sources of intelligence remain undeveloped.

Steve, aged seven, had been absent from school. On his return, conversation with his teacher went like this.

Teacher: 'I missed you yesterday, Steven. Where were you?'

Steve: 'I were poorly.'

Teacher: 'Where were you poorly?'

Steve: 'On't sofa.'

Teacher: 'I mean where on your body were you poorly?'

Steve: 'Gora pain in mi taboil' (ear hole, i.e. ear-ache).

Contrast this with Colin in similar circumstances.

Teacher: 'Hello, Colin. Where were *you* yesterday?'

Colin: 'I woke up feeling sick, with a pain in my head. My mother took my temperature and it was 104.'

Teacher: 'Did you have the doctor?'

Colin: 'Mother said she might ring him, but Gran said, "Oh, boys are up and down like yo-yos. I should give him a glass of Lucozade and keep him quiet".'

Teacher: 'And did that work?'

Colin: 'Yes. You see, I ate too much ice-cream. There's a lot of fat in ice-cream and the Lucozade helped me to digest it.'

Colin had his mother to himself for the first four years of his life. She talked to him and sang to him. Her voice was pleasing and Colin listened with great delight. She encouraged him in his vocal play and rewarded his efforts with her warm approval. She surrounded him with a wealth of happy experiences and a variety of play materials, and then provided him with good examples of speech with which to communicate his responses. Vocal interplay between himself and an attentive mother was the foundation of Colin's speech game. As he mastered his words, conversation with her helped him to acquire flexible modes of expression. Even when he was ill, she took the trouble to explain what she was doing with a thermometer and why she gave him Lucozade.

Steve competed for his mother's attention with two younger children. Older brothers and sisters looked after him as often as his mother did. He had no chance to develop a speech relationship with one person. Conversation in his home barely existed. If he was a nuisance he was cuffed or someone screamed 'Owd yer noise!' He learned to scream, too, because it was difficult to be heard against the background of perpetual noise from television, reinforced by the persistent clatter of life in a cluttered home. He didn't learn to speak well because he couldn't be heard and no one listened to him.

Many of our children come from homes where sentences are rarely spoken. Communication takes the form of grunts, ejaculations and gestures. A few words may be strung together without form or finish. They may be eked out by the repetition of 'You know', 'Like', 'Not it?', 'Because', et cetera. Information is incompletely conveyed. Ideas are disjointed. There are a few stock phrases from which the speaker selects one which seems to fit the situation. Speech is ugly and inadequate. In fact the only place in the home where articulate speech is heard is in the television corner. Much of this passes over the heads of the listeners because they lack the experience to provide the words with meaning. Books are rare and reading reduced to the newspaper that wraps the fish and chips.

An outstanding feature of the Plowden Report was the study it made of the effects of the child's home background and the particular aspects of home life that matter so much in the development of the child's linguistic skill.

School must help children like Steve to develop his speech if he is to have a normal tool for learning. This is not, however, the only handicap which faces such a child. The underprivileged home fosters other conditions which hinder the learning process in school.[12] In the clutter of Steve's home there is no privacy. Clothing is common property and each morning Steve dons an assortment of garments from the pile on the bedroom floor. There is no corner in the house he can call his own, nowhere to hide a present for Mum or a treasured possession, no place where he can be apart from all the others. Even the intimate life of his parents is thrust upon him before he is old enough to understand. Steve as an individual scarcely exists.

On entering school, Steve's greatest delight was to be given a chair he could call his own. Only those who earn in the home are entitled to a chair. With ten to feed at mealtimes, standing round the table is the only possible solution. Without good washing facilities, keeping clean in body and clothing is a problem and Steve's mum thinks twice before she changes his vest. Steve is socially handicapped, and the speech of other children is not readily available to help him with his own.

In homes like Steve's, living is a perpetual battle. There is no harmony in the home and tempers are short. A father who drinks as a means of escape may get into financial trouble. He may even land up in prison. Steve's emotional background is insecure. How can his teacher help him to express his experiences when they are ones he'd rather forget? How does he encourage him to recognise printed words when the emotional state of his mother has left him pathetically disintegrated? His teacher may make material provision to supplement his meagre experiences at home, but there is often little she can do to compensate for his arid emotional life. What conceptual foundation has Steve for the words his teacher can offer him? How is she going to fill in all the background to the words he will meet in books? Even the words of a first reader are outside his experience. Physically he could say them, but mentally he cannot recognise them at all.

In school Steve may ultimately learn a second language.

This will not in itself make learning easier for him. During his earyl years he has learned to respond and think through gestures and actions rather than through organised groups of words. He was taught to obey by commands, reinforced by physical action if necessary, rather than by reasoning: by 'Don't touch!' rather than by 'The teapot is hot and it's too heavy for you to lift. You might spill the hot tea if you try, and hot things can burn.' Language experience which steadily develops the linguistic skill of Colin would be unfamiliar to Steve. His teacher may be expecting him not merely to develop his use of language but to change his most deeply ingrained habits of thinking.

Linguistic change for a child tends to alienate him from his home background. His newly acquired language may not be socially acceptable at home. Either he must struggle with two different modes of expression and thought, or he must face the conflict of 'learning to speak above his station'. In underprivileged homes parents naturally feel an implied criticism if the speech they gave the child is not accepted in school.

What happens too often is that in school the child is taught to memorise word patterns by mechanical methods. Because the words mean little, what they convey means still less and is readily forgotten. Eleven-year-old Ida gained a Grammar School place from a single-class school in a colliery village. She was an intelligent child and she struggled valiantly to keep pace with her work. She confessed to another newcomer: 'It's all double dutch to me here. I don't know what the teachers are talking about half the time.' Her intellect remained untapped and she withdrew at the end of her first year, because she was unable to learn.

The young child's exploration depends initially on his own muscular activity. The intelligent baby may perfect the early stages of exploration on his own, but his discoveries can only become internalised with the use of language. However intelligent the baby may be, he depends on other people for his opportunity to learn language. He will only acquire the skill of words with the active help of another speaker. The child reared in a well-endowed home and attended by a communicative mother is given the best possible opportunity for developing speech and for exploring thought. The child brought up in the confusion of an underprivileged home may make intelligent attempts to talk which either go unrecognised or else are ignored.

When such a child comes into school, because he is inarticulate he may be misunderstood, even written off as dull. He will need a teacher who is sensitive to his mental and emotional state. He will need an abundance of sensory experiences and concrete situations to enlarge his conceptual understanding. He will need a one-to-one relationship with a person whose speech is mature. Above all he will need time to mature in speech and communication before he can benefit from more abstract forms of verbal learning.

The best possible remedy, perhaps, for inadequate early speech experience in the home is carefully planned pre-school education. Time, money and effort spent on educating the adolescent is wasted if the foundations are frail, and money spent on Nursery School education would give a profitable return to the nation in increased intelligence.

13

How children meet words in their environment

In every aspect of daily life words are brought to the child's attention. He uses them in speech and hears them spoken by others. He sees them used as labels on chocolate wrappers and salt packets, on streets, buses and shops. They give him directions such as up and down, in and out, hot and cold. They come to him in the form of stories to enjoy, as letters describing what is happening far away, and as news from all over the world. The child uses words on the telephone, he collects words about his discoveries, they form an essential part of his dramatic play. He hears his own words on the tape-recorder. He finds out about the people with whom he lives as often by using words as in any other way, and he learns much about his own person through the words of others. He uses words to shape and convey his thoughts and feelings. Through words he learns how to reason. Radio and television, gramophone records and books bring words to him from the minds of other people. Life at home and at school is permeated by words. In short, they are the life-blood of his learning.

In school, life revolves round what the teacher says. Words spoken by her will have a most profound influence on what the child does, how he does it and what he gains from doing it. Through her words he will learn about his own culture, its rules and attitudes, its aims and ideals. He will be shown how to behave in a group. What the teacher says to him will be eloquent of her own personality and characteristic of the society she represents.

The teacher's speech and her voice are her most powerful instruments, and the speech she uses out of school will influence her speech in it. In fact everything she experiences will influence her speech, because her voice is such an intimate part of her personality. Rough language, swearing, shouting and bawling can coarsen the voice. Even in schools where children learn mainly through their own activity, each child is subject to the sound of his teacher's voice for a large part of the day. He deserves good speech and a well-modulated voice. The teacher is apt to accept the quality of her own voice without question, forgetting that conscious effort can do much to improve it. Speech training may help a little, but clear thinking and sincerity of thought are perhaps the most effective means of improving the tone and quality of the human voice.

One of the teacher's main jobs is to help the child to build up and reinforce his vocabulary. She encourages the child to talk about what he is doing and so clarify his ideas. At the right moment she may provide him with a word which describes effectively what is happening. He may, for instance, stir sugar or salt in water until the water is clear. He will try to describe the process, using words he knows, saying, 'The sugar is all gone away'. If at that moment the adult supplies the word 'dissolve' he sees that it fits. He understands the word because he can endow it with meaning. He recognises it as appropriate because it crystallises his experiences and thought. He can then use it as an accurate description of what he saw happening.

When a child starts to include a word in his vocabulary, we can assume that the word means something to him. He may have heard the word 'friend' many times, but he will only start to use it at about the age of six when he has experienced the satisfaction of mutual exchange in a relationship. He will start to use words such as 'honesty' or 'truth' when social experiences have helped him to understand something of their moral implication. That he starts to use a word does not mean that he understands the full range of its meaning. Here again, his teacher can extend his experiences or link them with others. She may remind him, for instance, of the ways in which he used the words 'real', 'right', 'fair', and so on.

Words as sounds should predominate at this stage in the child's learning. Far too often it is words as visual patterns on paper which tend to become all-important, sometimes at the expense of the spoken word. We have come a long way from the day when the child only heard himself speak when he answered a question put by the teacher or articulated words from a reader. Few classrooms are silent; spontaneous speech is encouraged. Yet we still find anxious teachers thrusting words in print to the notice of children who cannot speak clearly, let alone shape words into sentences. A child cannot read until he has words to read with, for meaning resides initially in the spoken word.

When we ask a child to read, what are we expecting him to do? The pattern on paper is a symbol for a pattern of sound. The pattern of sound itself is only recognisable if it symbolises a familiar experience. The printed word 'cob' represents the spoken word 'cob'. Even when spoken it needs to be set in a sentence before we know whether it means a horse, a swan, a lump of coal, a head of corn, a little bread loaf, a kind of pipe, or a nut. A small child may have no experience of any of these objects, or he may know only a cob-nut. We present him with a very complicated process indeed when we ask him to read. We can train the child to make the appropriate sounds when we point to a printed word, but those sounds only become reading when they are attached to the child's personal experiences and so mean something to him. The accumulation of experiences takes time, and even when words are acquired in speech, still more time is needed to fill out their meaning. Unless this time is allowed to the child his reading will be very superficial or else will become mere articulation at parrot level.

Reading is only worth while when the words speak to us from the page. We recognise them because they remind us of an event or situation; they convey a message, conjure an image, start us thinking because they are interesting. They spark off a train of responses. They are not ends in themselves. Some teachers feel satisfied if the child merely makes the right sound. If words are not illuminated by the child's inner vision, they are useless to him and drill in articulating them is a waste of time. We might as well drill him into articulating Greek or Russian. If we try to teach word-recognition in a vacuum, we may very well end up with non-readers.

The most meaningful words to the child are his own, those he has selected from all the words in his environment as being of interest and use to him. Some of these words he will have in common with other children. Words such as mother, father, house, bed, dinner, are normally adopted by all children. But the child will also have a vocabulary arising from his individual environment. A child who comes into school from a golfing family will have different words from the child whose parents are circus people. Both sets of words are equally good because they are functional and we should take the child's home language into account when preparing material for him. When we help him to make his own reading material, through putting his spontaneous words on paper, we are fitting his use of the printed word into the pattern of his individual learning. Yet some teachers are guilty of introducing words in print which bear no relationship to the child's experiences, as the first step in recognising printed words. For example:

> The ram runs
> Help!

The ram runs at the hen
Help!

What does the child from the urban home, or indeed from a literate home in any locality, make of this?

That we need to add words to the child's vocabulary is true, but we add words in action before we present the symbols of those actions to the child.

We may plan to extend the child's use of adjectives. A child tells you that tissue paper is 'soft like skin' and we know that he is ready to understand texture words. We set out opportunities for him to experience various surfaces . . . a piece of bark, a polished wooden bowl, a shell, a piece of rough stone. We encourage the child to handle these objects and talk about them. He feels the need for words which describe differences in these surfaces, and we give him the words rough and smooth to add to the words hard and soft he already knows. Later, when he meets such words in print they will be associated with the feelings he has experienced.

Likewise the child exploring the use of his body in movement feels his way through such words as 'fast', 'slow', 'crawl', 'stretch', 'swirling and twirling'. His imagination is fired and his words are tinged with poetry.

When the child watches the behaviour of dry sand, he learns something about 'sift', 'dredge', 'drift', 'pile' or 'cascade', and using these words is part of his active relationship with them.

While the child is building with bricks he will learn to associate such words as 'cube', 'cylinder' and 'sphere' with what his hands and his eyes have taught him about the shape of his bricks.

It is through such activities in which words and experiences become inextricably interwoven that the child grows to find in language a most perfect tool for his learning.

14

Listening and speaking

The child's first experience of speech is listening to the speech of his parents, and learning speech plays an essential part of his early life in the home. Although the quality of their speech varies considerably, all children accomplish much during the first five years of life. School will offer them many opportunities for extending their speech, largely through sharing 'speech' experiences with others. Listening will continue to play a leading part in speech development.

Even the child from the articulate home still needs a great deal of help with his words, in the form of speech, before he can be helped to use them in other ways. Unless the child talks, no one knows what kind of help he needs, and teachers in the modern Infant School find many ways of encouraging the child to talk. Children for much of the time move freely about the room and when they do sit down, as often as not they face one another. Learning is approached through doing, and the common interests the children find in their jobs provide topics for discussion with other children and with the teacher. There are many interesting experiments to make, and discoveries excite speech as a way of expressing these experiences to others. The whole atmosphere of the school fosters communication and much of this exchange takes the form of spoken words.

When a child has something to say he needs an audience. Other children may listen to him, sometimes he acts as his own audience, but what he likes best of all is an adult to talk to. The greatest help an adult can give a child is to listen to him, letting him open up his mind and shape it through putting his ideas into words. The adult who listens is allowed to reach into the child's mind and feel his way round the child's understanding. We know, by what he says, what interests the child, how he feels about things, and how far he is able to reason. His speech is a good guide to his personality and his intellectual capacity. How much more do we find out about a child's thought-processes in handling number relationships by encouraging him to talk about them, than we do if we show him how to manipulate numbers mechanically on paper.

The main problem for the teacher is the number of children she wants to listen to. They need listening to one at a time. Ten minutes spent with one child may last him for a week, but most children need this kind of help daily, almost hourly.

The teacher's time can be eked out by students on teaching practice, by visitors to the school, or by ancillary helpers such as school secretaries and caretakers. Some fortunate teachers have assistants such as trainees from Nursery nurses' courses or classroom helpers. One school invited mothers to share the work of the teachers for a short time each day. The head-mistress could regard her listening ear as the main part of her job in her capacity as leading teacher of the school. In many Infant Schools the headmistress makes personal contact with each child in the school, every day, her primary concern. These headmistresses do far more for the child's linguistic development in this way than they would by hearing slow readers labour over dull pages.

From time to time the listening adult joins in with the conversation and leads the child towards greater precision in his speech. Sometimes the child's speech is faulty. Defects may

85

be due to faulty speech organs, cleft palate, hare lip, or enlarged tonsils. Often poor speech is the result of bad speech habits such as slurring, unfinished words, and so on. Emotional problems may affect speech; stuttering and stammering, for instance, can be due to lack of confidence and are often the result of parental pressure. Speech errors and speech disorders reduce the child's chance of communicating effectively, and they should be remedied at the earliest possible moment. Many local authorities employ a skilled speech therapist who will advise and assist if children are referred to her notice. Poor pronunciation and inadequate speech can have severe effects on the development of the child's personality and his progress in school. Responsible adults must get skilled help for the child if he is to use his opportunities to the full.[13]

The child needs to speak, but he needs to listen as well. He learns to speak through listening, and listening is where language experience begins. Educating the child to listen is as important as educating him to speak. How many of us, as adults, are really good listeners? The good listener can often offer more help to a person in trouble than any amount of do-gooding can. A good lecture is useless unless the listener can listen creatively.

How often do we misunderstand because our ears and our minds have let us down? How often do we miss completely some of the loveliest of sound experiences, because we hear without listening? We never learned how to listen and much in life passes us by.

Listening to stories plays an essential part in the life of the child and the pleasure of the story itself is not its only benefit. In a story, or in poetry, human experience is interpreted. The writer uses words with skill, economy and beauty, weaving his material into artistic form. Carefully chosen and well presented, stories and poetry have a powerful purpose in education.

The young child listening can explore situations which supplement or extend his own experiences. He can learn more about himself, or identify himself with the hero who meets and solves familiar problems. He can find relief from emotional strain. He can wing away into the world of his imagination. Many stories convey to him the attitudes of his society and the cultural beliefs of the race he belongs to. Words capture him and compel him to listen. They take him by the hand and lead him into the world of fresh delight, where meaning is conveyed by simile, metaphor and image.

Stories for the young child are often better told than read If the teacher has made the story her own, she can dispense with the barrier of a book between herself and the child. She is free to watch his face as she tells the story. She knows by the expression on his face where she needs to enlarge the meaning or modify the narrative. She is sensitive to his reactions and adjusts her story accordingly. Between them, child and teacher create the story. The intimate peace of storytime depends on the teacher's sensitivity to her material and to her children. She chooses her story as much because she loves it as because she thinks it might interest her children. She prepares it with care and creates the right atmosphere before she shares the experience with her listeners.

In story or poetry, the rhythm and beauty of the words hold the child with their magic. Children retain much of what they hear and want to hear it repeated. They may memorise whole poems in this way. Rote learning of poetry for the sake of repeating it has little value, but a mind stored with poetic phrases or sentences will lead to the full appreciation of the artistic use of words. We encourage good listening by giving children things which are worth listening to, and in Chapter 19 the literary value of stories will receive our attention.

A modern aid in the classroom is the tape-recorder and many Infant teachers find this a valuable aid to good speech. In one classroom the teacher first recorded the spontaneous speech of the children as they chatted in the Wendy House or made fabric pictures and models together. They were unaware, until she played the tape to them, of her activity. They were delighted to hear themselves speak and wanted to know 'how it worked'. Once the children were thoroughly familiar with the equipment, their teacher recorded their speech in a number of ways – reading their own stories and poems, telling stories, describing experiences or experiments, and so on. She then recorded their early morning chatter of 'news' items from home. One child, hearing her recorded version of a 'Thunderbirds' programme, said critically, 'It wasn't the same really' (i.e. her report was inaccurate).

The teacher also recorded a story composed and told by Roy, an articulate boy of seven, and accounts by other children of books they had read in the library corner. After playing these records back to the children, the teacher typed them out. She pasted the typescript of Roy's story in a book which he illustrated. The accounts of library books were also pasted into a 'Book about our Books'. In this way story books and book reviews became part of the class reading material. Such books which contained the children's own words were highly popular.

In another classroom was a boy of seven who showed little interest in reading. Eric's teacher encouraged him to tell her about the things he liked doing. She taped his responses, and when he heard himself speak Eric volunteered, 'I can tell you a lot more'. His teacher took some photographs of Eric which fitted what he told her. She then made a book using the photographs and a typescript of the tape-recording. She left the 'Book about Eric' in a prominent position on her desk. Eric saw the book with a photograph of himself and his name on the front. His curiosity made him anxious to find out what was in the book and he pestered anyone who could help him. The book proved a breakthrough for his reading skill.

The telephone is an interesting piece of equipment to be

88

found in most schools and the job of answering it is highly prized. In some schools children sign up on a rota for telephone duty when the headmistress is abroad in the classrooms. An attractive book-corner occupies the attendant in between calls. Although the attendant may only ask the caller to wait while he fetches the headmistress, this experience helps to emphasise the importance of speech and gives rise to some interesting observations.

'The lady said she was in another school. How can I hear her all that far away?'

'The gentleman said I was a clever little boy. How did he know when he couldn't see me?'

'It was a lady. She sounded like somebody's Gran.'

Field telephone systems have been installed in some schools, so that communication between classrooms is established. The speech of many children improves tremendously and inarticulate children are often surprisingly liberated through this impersonal medium.

In ways such as these children are made more aware of their own speech and of the need for accuracy and good pronunciation. They are encouraged to improve their speech through conscious effort. They learn to realise its function in communication and to see the link between spoken and written words.

Most children are accustomed to the speech of radio and television broadcasters. In some homes unfortunately such speech is ignored and becomes merely background noise. We can use this material most effectively by encouraging children to listen and watch with discrimination. We can know and discuss with them suitable programmes, not only those specifically designed for children, but certain serials, magazine programmes and documentaries which we know by their time of showing children are likely to watch. We may not approve of some of the programmes, but we cannot avoid knowing that they have a powerful impact on children and

89

we can turn them to good account by helping children to develop powers of discrimination.

The teacher's own speech and how she uses it interpenetrate every aspect of the child's linguistic development in school. It will influence the child incidentally throughout his relationship with her. Sometimes she gives him the benefit of her own speech example by telling him about her own experiences. Sometimes she reads to him from a book a story or a poem or information which interests him. This reading to the child starts in the home, when mother or father reads a bedtime story from his new Christmas book. It should continue at least through the Primary School. 'Reading to' is a link between talking and reading. It helps the child to bridge the gap between the spoken words he hears and the pattern those words make on paper.

In the modern world mechanical sound is becoming a threat and we grow increasingly conscious of the need to reduce harsh sound to a minimum. Even musical sound, if it creates a permanent background as it can with television and radio in every home, is capable of reducing man's sensitivity to the things he hears. It is becoming more and more a responsibility of the teacher to help children to retain and develop their sensitivity to sound, particularly to the sound of the human voice, and so to maintain their delight in the joy of listening.

15

Becoming familiar with words on paper

Printed words have been part of the child's environment since he was born. Many children of three can recognise the name of their street, the place where the bus stops, the notice which says Daddy can't smoke. The initial stages of learning to read are something the child shares with parents and others who love him: it is a happy and joyous experience.

The four-year-old fetches the *Radio Times* so that father can find out when their favourite programme will be on. He knows which record plays the Toy Symphony. He recognises the difference between Crispies and Cornflakes on the packets which look alike. He can recognise the shop which is 'Boots', even in a strange town. The letter from sister Jenny tells mother what Jenny is doing, even when she's away at college, and with mother's help he can sign his name at the bottom of the letter mother writes back. Helped by a sympathetic adult, he makes these discoveries daily.

How much each child knows about words on entering school depends on intellect, the physical ability to see and hear, the range and quality of his experiences, and the interest and attitude in his home background. Some children of five can read and enjoy a story; some have no idea how to handle a book.

Sheila came from a professional home. On her first day in

school she produced a Bible from her new satchel and offered to read from it. She turned to the Song of Solomon and read: 'For, lo, the winter is passed, the rain is over and gone, the flowers appear on the earth, the time of the singing of birds is come and the voice of the turtle is heard in our land'. She read it beautifully and with feeling for the words.

Janice lived on a new housing estate. Her mother always bought a woman's magazine every week. Janice knew the magazine told mother how to make a delicious chocolate cake. She couldn't read herself, but she understood the purpose of reading and soon started to ask 'What does this say?'

Stephen came from an illiterate home, and books meant little to him. He went into the book-corner and tore up one of the new picture books.

Each of these children has different needs. In some cases curiosity about words and a desire to read them has not been stimulated by the home background. The teacher must first stimulate an interest in words and then develop that interest.

The provision of books of the right kind in both the home and the school is essential. Even then it is not enough. A child needs to know that adults themselves enjoy and respect books. Of course the teacher loves books, but she needs to let the child see that she does, and the place given to books in the classroom is the first indication of this to the child.

Parents and teachers today have a wonderful selection of books at their disposal. Covers are attractive and introduce the child to the contents of the book, but the reading matter inside is even more important and every book should be read by parent or teacher before it is released to children.

Reading material should be related to the immediate experiences of children; it should be well illustrated with pictures of good quality; the print should be clear, and the vocabulary good and closely related to that of the child. The first books a child meets will colour his future attitude to books and reading.

In school some of these books will be displayed on racks or tables in a corner of the classroom. Small comfortable chairs, flowers on the table, and the feeling that this is a pleasant, peaceful place will encourage the child to go there and enjoy the experience.

In other parts of the room books will serve a different purpose. Where there are objects of interest on the investigation table or displays are made of natural materials or the work of an artist, appropriate reference books will be associated with each of the exhibitions. With the help of the teacher or a friend a child can then find answers to questions stimulated by the displays. Even if he is only told what it says in the book, as the teacher turns the pages he will associate meaning with printed words as she shares the book with him. Reading *with* the teacher is an excellent help to most children at some stage in the development of their reading skill.

Opportunities for social play in school encourage the development of speech. In school the child has many experiences which stir him into telling someone about them. The teacher gives him writing materials, paper, crayons and paint, so that he can express his thoughts and feelings on paper, either in the form of pictures or in words.

One teacher took a series of photographs of the children at work. She pasted these into a book and let the children chatter about them; then she wrote what they had said beneath the pictures, thus making their first reading book.

Children can cut out pictures from magazines and paste them into scrap books. The teacher can then write for each child the comments he makes about his pictures, and he can copy the words beneath hers.

A rota is required for taking turns in the sand tray or painting-corner. The teacher can show the child how to write his own name, so that he can sign up for himself on the appropriate list.

In short, she uses every opportunity in the child's day-today living to help him to understand the value of reading. In this way she establishes the right approach. A good attitude on the part of the child provides a fertile background for more systematic help, and very soon the teacher can link the spoken and written word in more definite ways.

A neatly printed notice, for example, reminds the child where to hang his rubber apron; his name is written above his cloakroom peg. John made a clay bowl and displayed it on the shelf reserved for children's work, and the teacher labelled it: 'John made this bowl'.

In dramatic play children will imitate the adult, and the teacher can help them make out bills, invitations to parties, and so on.

On one occasion a parcel of patchwork pieces was brought for the sewing-table, and five children selected choice pieces and pasted them into a book. With the aid of the teacher they wrote their impressions of these materials, e.g. 'Silk is thin. I like feeling it. It is soft. It looks like the Spring Festival'. As a result of investigation, a child may make herself a book. One day the teacher gave Janet a paper serviette for the Wendy House, printed with the French words for numbers. Janet asked the teacher to explain the words and was thrilled to discover that people in other countries write numbers in different ways. With the aid of reference books she compiled her own book on 'The Way Other People Write Numbers'. Most children also like to make books about themselves, their families and playmates.

In these ways and many others, the child is exploring man's use of words in the routine of his daily life. During the process of imposing order on his world the child feels the need to fit these printed symbols into the pattern. As his mind becomes more firmly structured he recognises the need to understand printed symbols as an important part of being able to understand his environment.

In the early stages understanding is intuitive, and for some children intuitive thinking will make the symbols comprehensible. Most children, however, turn to the adult sooner or later for help in analysing and interpreting them. It is at this point that we recognise the child as being ready to learn to read.[14] The child's curiosity about visible symbols is aroused and his intense interest at this stage renders him highly teachable. This interest in symbols is not restricted to words in print. It extends to many other symbols on paper and the recognition of numbers, musical symbols, diagrams and maps grows alongside his reading. They are, in fact, part of his learning to read.

The child may be sufficiently aware of the reading process to ask the adult: 'Will you teach me to read?' Most children, however, are not capable of expressing their need so explicitly. They show us in other ways that they are ready and the sensitive parent or teacher can recognise the signs.

A child may ask: 'What does this say?' He may reproduce isolated words amongst his scribble, or may point them out on a birthday card or in a book and ask for an explanation. Some will notice the initial sounds of words, or the recurrence of sounds as parts of words. Penny was interested in the illustrated dictionary in the reading-corner. She was delighted to find her own name beside the picture of a penny. She then pointed to other words on the same page in great excitement. 'This starts like my name. That starts like my name . . .' She was told the sound 'p' and spent the next half-hour finding all the words which included 'p'.

At first for the majority of children the single word is only part of a whole situation. It may act as a link in a chain of activity, e.g. 'We must drive in through the right gate, Daddy. This is the one which says "In".' Children will be interested in a complete page of reading if it tells them how the spider makes his web. Many children are unable for quite a long time to isolate separate words or to see differences between them. A child can of course be taught to recognise separate

95

sounds and words, but he may not connect them with reading at all.

Most children, then, begin by reading simple sentences which have meaning, and only when the idea of reading itself is established do they analyse sentences into words. Beryl, at the age of four and a half, was devoted to her 'Mother Goose Nursery Rhyme Book'. At frequent intervals she would turn to 'Old Mother Hubbard' and pester her older sister, 'Let me read it to you'. Her patient older sister would listen as Beryl burbled through the nursery rhyme, following the words generally with her finger.

One day she forgot her older sister. She stared at the page in great surprise and then, plucking each word separately from the page, read slowly: 'Old . . . Mother . . . Hubbard . . .' Her excitement and delight sustained her right through the rhyme. The words had spoken to her from the page. They had revealed their secret. In a moment of insight she had accomplished the first major step in her interpretation of printed words.

For many children the process is slower, but it need never become laboured if we let each child make his discoveries at his own pace and give him only the help he is needing. Over-helping will slow his pace, make him feel inadequate, deprive him of the joy of making his own discoveries, and even turn his joy into dislike and sometimes fear.

At a later stage, when reading ideas and attitudes are established, phonic units may help a child and he can use them as clues to solve his word problems. Some children 'tumble' to an understanding of phonic units and enjoy pointing out separate sounds within a word. But not all children find an analytical approach to word recognition helpful. Some teachers provide the child with the whole word each time he is stuck until he becomes independent. Teachers who have helped hundreds of children through their early stages of reading would find it difficult to say precisely how they helped or how the child bridged the gap between spoken and printed word. Most would agree that they surrounded the child with all they felt would help him, offering different aids to individual children, and that in the end it was the child who accomplished the feat for himself.

The adult who is sensitive to the needs of the child as a whole person, and who is tuned in to the developing mind of the child, can give him a lot of help when he is learning to read. The emphasis must be on the child's active learning rather than on her teaching by instructing him. Some teachers feel guilty if the child has 'learned to read by himself'. They don't feel they have earned their money unless they have 'taught' him. Much of the systematic help we try to give the child is very misguided. Sometimes the child is hindered rather than helped by the material and methods we use.

The mind of the active five- and six-year-old is rich with words of his own. From his various experiences he has acquired exciting words such as 'speed', 'crash', 'blaze', 'fire-engine', or lovely sounding words such as 'stars', 'darkness', 'space', 'Martians'. He does not need two-dimensional paper pictures to illustrate these words for him. They are already illuminated by his own inner vision. The very saying of them lights his mind, for these words are the material of his mind. They are the ones he is ready to recognise in printed form.

What do we do? Some teachers help the child to meet these words in printed form by writing them down for him and helping him to write them himself. These teachers may then type out the words so that they resemble the words in printed books. Many teachers, however, ignore these words completely. They present the child with a collection of words thought up by a person who has never met either the child or his teacher, and then expect him to be interested in them.

Because the words are unfamiliar they are illustrated by flat paper pictures, which often provide little clue to their meaning. The first stages of existing reading schemes, even those published by reputable firms, could scarcely be classified as good literature. Some are sheer gibberish and an insult to the child. The child deserves material of literary value as his introduction to the printed word.

Most teachers would agree with these comments and would still persist in using 'First Stages'. They seem to provide the teacher with a sense of security. She feels assured that she has done what she can when she has given the child his daily dose of a controlled vocabulary.

In some schools books from reading schemes are introduced to the child as soon as he enters, and teachers are preoccupied with hearing children 'read' or practise the skill of word recognition even before the child knows what reading is about.

A teacher of children from professional homes once confessed: 'I give each child a reader as soon as he comes into school. He keeps it in his tidy box. When mother asks anxiously, "Are you on to a reader yet, dear?" the child can set her mind at rest and I can get on with the business of teaching him to read.' Perhaps the main purpose of readers is to allay the anxiety of parents and teachers. In Chapter 17 we will consider the value of reading schemes more closely.

There are four recognised methods of giving systematic help with word recognition. The alphabet method, by which children use letter names to spell out words, was used in many Infant Schools during the last century. This is virtually obsolete. In the phonic method, children are taught the sounds of letters or groups of letters as clues to recognising words. Unfortunately the English language contains many words which cannot be deciphered in this way. Words which can be sounded phonetically make dull reading material: 'the bad fox is sad' will scarcely interest a young child. In the 'whole word' or 'look and say' method children memorise the whole word. Any words of interest to the child can be used, but it provides no clues for unfamiliar words and the child depends on the adult to tell him each word. The same principle applies to the sentence method, but here he is told the whole sentence. Reading material is based on the child's own experiences and this procedure helps him to read such sentences as 'John will give out milk today'.

Few teachers use one of these methods exclusively. Some use a combination and adjust the method to the type of child. Many teachers proceed to help the child without reference to particular methods at all; they simply offer such help as seems appropriate and encourage the child to learn as naturally as possible. They see the recognition of words as a stage in the structuring of his mind. Their approach is based on Piaget's view of the child's development. The view a teacher holds of education is clearly reflected in the way she approaches the teaching or learning of reading.

Once printed words are familiar most children find them interesting for their own sake. They enjoy playing with them, grouping them into families, seeing little words in big words, finding words which begin in the same way and so on. They enjoy collecting words: colour words, doing words, words about water, words which sound lovely. In this way the use of dictionaries grows alongside creative writing. A child's dictionary book is simple at first – merely a plain book in which the teacher writes the word the child needs for his writing. Later the words can be classified in groups or in alphabetical order. Clearly the development of writing and reading is inseparable, and the child's command of words grows through his own use of them.

Learning to read is a continuous process. Except in a very few extremely abnormal cases all children can learn to read, but the pace must suit the child, and the Junior and Secondary Schools must take the responsibility of continuing the teaching of reading. The child who gets there first is not necessarily the best reader, and many children who make no real start until they are seven or eight can rival the early starter at the age of ten. A person has seventy-odd years to devote to his reading. We can allow a child five or six years of doing things which enrich words with meaning before we subject him to any form of direct tuition. Above all, the attitude of the adults who help the child is far, far more important than the methods used to instruct him.

16

The joy of reading

Although books have existed since the fifteenth century, the practice of printing them for children is a comparatively recent development. The idea that children should enjoy books scarcely occurred to our forefathers, and until the seventeenth century the only books printed for them were school textbooks and books of etiquette. Puritan writers such as John Bunyan and James Janeway, whose aim was to 'rescue' children, were amongst the first to write for them, and *Pilgrim's Progress* appeared in 1675.

John Locke in the late seventeenth century thought children should learn to read and have suitable books from which to do so. He was concerned about the grave shortage of material for children. Adult books such as Defoe's *Robinson Crusoe* (1719) and Swift's *Gulliver's Travels* (1726) were to become popular with children, but it wasn't until the rise of the middle classes in the latter part of the eighteenth century that the idea of children's books became established. The first bookshop for children was opened by John Newbery in 1745.

Early books for children such as Samuel Richardson's *Pamela* were neither suitable nor attractive. The late eighteenth century found cheap books circulating amongst ordinary people, who were now becoming literate, at $\frac{1}{4}$d to 1d per volume. Most of these were of poor quality and have not lasted. Alphabet books were popular. Fairy tales were frowned upon; John Locke had thought them 'perfectly useless trumpery'. Nursery rhymes were acceptable, and family stories with a moral in each chapter, such as Martha Mary Butt's *History of the Fairchild Family*, were considered improving for children.

It wasn't until the nineteenth century that good writers were prepared to write for children. The population was becoming better educated and a breakthrough in children's literature included Lewis Carroll's *Alice in Wonderland*, Charles Kingsley's *Water Babies*, and Louisa Alcott's *Little Women*. Before the First World War we find a first golden age of children's literature. Kipling's *Kim* (1901), Kenneth Grahame's *Wind in the Willows* (1908), and Barrie's *Peter Pan* (1906) were books which are still popular today.

The First World War affected children's literature through the loss of writers and through paper shortage. Quantities of books of poor quality followed the war; the few exceptions included A. A. Milne's *Winnie the Pooh* (1926), the *William* books of Richmal Crompton (1920s), and P. L. Travers's *Mary Poppins* (1930s).

The Second World War brought its restrictions, but today we have entered a second golden age. Children are recognised as prolific readers. Science fiction, school stories, novels, plays and poetry flood the market. Publishers employ every technique to make books attractive and educative. Children are encouraged to read by the books themselves. We are as concerned about the material we offer children as we are about the way we help them acquire the skill of reading. What they read is as important as how they read it.

Nowadays we expect every citizen to read. Literature of all kinds is available at prices which meet the pocket of the poorest person. We expect to find the printed word in many forms and books in every home. We regard the acquisition of reading as an essential skill.

The way we teach reading is often influenced by methods of instruction employed by our forefathers. A brief consideration of the development of these methods helps to explain the unfortunate attitude on the part of many parents and teachers when helping children today.

One of the earliest aids for children was the hornbook. This at first was a thin piece of horn and later a piece of paper, 3 inches by 4 inches, fastened to a thin board. At the top of the paper the alphabet in capital and small letters appeared. Then came the vowels, double lines of ab, eb, ib, and so on, and the benediction. The Lord's Prayer or roman numerals occupied the remaining space.

The Primer was originally a book of private devotions: the Lord's Prayer, the Ten Commandments, and the Psalms. It was inexpensive and intended to help poor people to learn how to read their Bibles. The alphabet was frequently included. This is why elementary books for the use of children became known as primers.

People in the seventeenth century thought of the child's mind as a *tabula rasa*, on which patterns of learning were etched by instruction. The idea of the mind as a developing aspect of the person, which matured stage by stage into its adult structure, was considered by only a few people like Comenius and Pestalozzi. The significance of maturation was quite unthought of, and meaningless sounds and symbols were instilled in unformed minds in the hope that the child would learn to understand them by memorising them. Picture alphabets and rhyming jingles were thought to be an introduction to reading, as in the following cases:

'In Adam's fall   'Zaccheus he
We sinned all.'   Did climb the Tree
'Heaven to find   Our Lord to see.'
The Bible mind.'

Speaking of elementary school education in England, John Locke informs us that in 1690 'The method to adhere to is the ordinary road of the Hornbook Primer, Psalter, Testament and Bible; these are the only books used to engage the liking of children and tempt them to read'.

There were three reading classes in the school. The beginners joined the Psalter class. The Testament class followed and the Bible class was the final goal. A child went through two chapters at each session. He had to spell out the words in the section read.

Spelling books became popular in 1750 and for seventy-five years they proved practically the only source of instruction for school children.

In more recent years help given to children in school has ranged from instruction of the whole class to individual help. Few schools would expect children to chant in unison as the teacher points out words on a blackboard, but one can still find schools where reading round the class is practised, and in many schools children in small ability groups are expected to read in turn. Sometimes silent reading takes place as a special exercise. Comprehension of the matter read may be tested.

In many Infant Schools teachers hear children read aloud individually. The material they read is as often from their own writing as from printed books. Teachers find assurance in hearing the child articulate the words and use this as a measure of the child.s skill. Some schools have more confidence in making words a vital part of the child's life and teachers assess the child's skill by what he absorbs rather than by his ability to recognise and articulate each word. Ultimately reading aloud is largely discarded and one wonders whether some children ever need to do it. There can be no greater delight for a teacher of young children than to find a child chuckling to himself over a book or lost in the world of a story he can read to himself, unless it be the child who, independent of his teacher's help, can satisfy his curiosity through information he collects from books. In whatever way we help the child to acquire reading skill, the end-product should always be silent and fluent.

Today we have at our disposal a wealth of material. Much of it is good, some of it excellent, but there is still a distressing amount of trash amongst printed material for children. Gimmicky books, flashy jackets and covers which are little guide to the contents, and an indifferent or inaccurate text often tempt the adult to pay up. There is a tendency also to illustrate books so profusely that nothing is left to the child's imagination. Pictures should illuminate, not dominate. A good story will weave its own pictures in the mind of the reader. Some books, of course, depend more on picture than text to convey their message. Here again, pictures should be authentic in detail and well produced. Some products are an insult to children. The selection of books will be considered further in Chapter 17.

Only material of high quality is suitable for the young reader. Books should tempt a child to explore and then satisfy his curiosity with their delight. Reading is an exploratory activity. It should be a joyful experience at all times. It can be shared with another person or it can be individual, but it should never be a form of drudgery. At all stages the attitude of adult and child to his reading will colour the learning books offer.

17

The literary value of books available

The use the adult makes of words and the type of literature he appreciates depends on the words he has met and the ways he has seen them used. The words he first meets as a child remain his words for the rest of his life. Many of our children meet words used well in print for virtually the first time when they enter school.

When we select material to put before children we must ask a number of questions. What do we look for in a book for children? What happens to books in schools? And, most important of all, are the words used the right ones?

Certain principles guide our selection of books of any kind for children. They should be well printed on paper of good quality. The print should be clear and large enough to suit the visual acuity of the age-group; illustrations should be authentic. Photographs are more informative than drawings and diagrams. They can be used to break up the text into digestible pieces. Whether the child can read or not, large slabs of unbroken text are discouraging.

Books make their first appeal to the eye. Colour is important, but we should not suppose that young children always like gaudy colours. The work of a good artist always appeals and crude bright colour which catches the adult eye is not necessarily the child's choice. Some children indeed prefer black-and-white etchings or charcoal designs. Not all children need to find stories profusely illustrated, for the story which is well written conjures its own pictures in the mind of the child. Poetry in particular should be sensitively illuminated. The mind of the child is alive with vivid pictures, and he does not need the imagination of others to bring stories to life for him.

While books need strong covers and should be reasonably durable, they should not be too much so. They should be used with respect because their quality is good, but they should be used to death and then replaced. We should never find in school either books preserved in their original splendour or books so dog-eared that they become distasteful.

A book should also appeal to the hands. The shape, size and weight of books are important factors. Giant, showy books persuade money from the pockets of adults, but the child will love neat, well-designed books which will rest on his knee and sometimes the small book he can hold in his fingers. Books with plastic or varnished pages may be strong, but they rarely appeal to children's fingers. On the other hand, a polythene jacket to protect an attractive book-cover heightens its attraction.

Very often parents and even teachers buy a book because the cover is promising. Every book should be read before it is purchased. Parents welcome the help of the teacher in selecting books for presents, and a school display of suitable books just before Christmas will guide parents into spending money wisely.

Most local authorities try to be generous with book allowances and the money is spent on a wide range of individual books rather than on sets of books. Children are learning to read from books which interest and inform. The skilful teacher can guide the child towards finding what he needs in books he can understand. The child may require help here and there with the words, but he accomplishes the basic stages of learning to read by reading from good material.

We still find in many schools that books from reading schemes are used to introduce the child to words in print and then to give him practice in word recognition. The guarantee of a controlled vocabulary fed to the child in graded steps is the absolute antithesis of the true aims of reading. It may provide a sense of security for those teachers who believe that, if they take the child methodically through the stages prescribed, then the miracle of reading is assured.

Try reading aloud from cover to cover a book from the early stages of any reading scheme. Is this the way children speak? Is this material calculated to entice the child to try to master the skill which will help him to read more of it? Does it even make sense? How many of these early stages can compete with the wide range of attractive books available? The more advanced stages of most reading schemes contain very good stories and deserve an honoured place in the book-corner, but too many of the books which are intended to serve as the child's introduction to reading are gibberish and more likely to put him off reading than to encourage him to go further.

The child has words of his own. When he hears the words he loves his mind illuminates them with living pictures from his own experiences. Some words are common to all children, but each child has his own collection of words. It may be excavator, lorry, and tractor which interest John, and ribbon, dolly, and satin which interest Peggy. We should use the material in the child's own mind if we want him to read in the full meaningful sense of the word. Ways in which we can help children to read their own words will be discussed in the next chapter. Words from the mind of another person will interest him later, but to meet his own friendly words in another shape makes reading a natural development of his own speech, and this is what reading is.

Many children come into school from homes where books are scarce or non-existent. They need help in their use of books. and introducing a child to his books is the first step towards helping him to use them effectively. However well books are displayed and organised, it is not fair to expose the child to them unaided. He needs to learn from the adult how to respect and handle them.

The teacher lets the child see how she uses books and how she cares for them. For instance she may share the unpacking of new books with children singly or in small groups. 'Here is a lovely new book. We're the first people to open it and look inside. What do you think it will be about? The little yellow duck is funny, isn't he? Shall we see what he has been doing?' By being introduced to a book in this way, the child is given some idea as to its contents before it goes into the book rack.

The teacher may read a story or perhaps a poem from a chosen book which she then leaves for the children to investigate. She may help a child to find an answer to his questions by sharing an informative book with him. She makes books for the children or helps them to make books themselves, and these, too, take their place amongst those purchased. A child who has made a book is aware of the care and effort needed to produce one. Attitudes of delight and respect are established in him right from the start.

Books should hold a prominent and honoured position in any school and in every classroom. Their position and the way they are arranged influence the use made of them by children and teachers. Books tightly packed behind glass doors with only their spines visible through the windows do not encourage anyone to explore them. Books isolated in a central part of the school may be sought after by older children, but the young child needs his books around him in the room while he works.

Books should be displayed with their covers showing. Racks made for this purpose can be purchased, but suitable display shelves can be improvised and need cost little. Wooden slats nailed to the back of a cupboard with curtain wire to support the books, plywood nailed to one side of a wooden clothes-horse, again with curtain wire to support the books, tables or shelves with metal clips to hold some books upright, peg-board with metal clips – all are ways of arranging books so that they can be seen and easily reached.

Often displays of materials are associated with appropriate reference books in which children can find out about the things which interest them. Books on a table in a corner screened off from the rest of the room encourage quiet reading. The books may carry some guiding mark which indicates the difficulty of the material. 'L' for learner or 'A' for advanced reader may help children to select a suitable book. Flowers and comfortable chairs add to the appeal of reading-corners. Some books may be displayed farther afield, in a peaceful corner of the school hall or in a spare classroom. Here children from all parts of the school can share books, often helping one another to read them. As a child gains confidence he may take a book he is writing to complete it where the sources of information are available.

The use children are making of books in a school is a safe guide to their skill in reading. If a child can find his own answers from books, if he can enjoy in private a good story or commit to mind the words of a poem, if he can record his discoveries and write his own story, need we ask him to read aloud to us? Does it matter whether he can recognise each separate word in a book or whether he reads all the words? Need children plod and stumble, sound by sound, through what they read? Is it not the meaning behind the words they are after? Can we not let children enjoy books in their own way, helping them to decipher words when they need it? Do they all need the same kind of help? We should not, it is true, forget the need for thorough reading, for extracting the full meaning from what is read, but doesn't this depend more on the appeal of the content than on the visual recognition of the words?

Tony was a quiet child of six. He stood patiently in the teacher's small circle, listening to his friends as they read aloud in halting voices. When his turn came he sounded each word carefully and completed correctly the sentence he was expected to read. The group changed and Tony slipped his reader away in his tidy box. He then retired to the book-corner and was immediately caught up in the words of his favourite story book.

The teacher knew Tony could read. 'But I have to make sure,' she explained, 'that he isn't missing any words out, or getting some of them wrong.' Would that teacher read each word separately, or read every word of the novel she took to bed at the end of the day? How can we expect children to become good readers if we teach them to read with the brakes on?

A visitor to another Infant School was asked by a child of five: 'Do you want to see the head teacher? She's Miss Digby and she's in the room with her name on the door. I've just seen her and she's given me this new book out of the box she's unpacking. It's all about a baby seal who lived in a nursery bed and had to learn how to swim. He had a white coat before he got his seal coat and I'm taking the book to my teacher for her to read it to me again.'

In this school books lined the walls of the corridor. A group of children were gathered round a table in the foyer. They were comparing the moss against the stones in a shallow dish with pictures in a book. One child read from the book to the other children.

Classroom doors stood open. Inside each room children could be seen making scrap books and picture books, writing stories, making books about space travel, doll's clothing, and picnics in the park. One group were making jam tarts, following the recipe printed in a book. Some boys in the hall were following the instructions they had found in a book for making a water organ. One child stood in front of the piano fingering out a tune from the simple chart made by her teacher. Another child was absorbed in merely turning the pages of a book in the book-corner, because this was the stage she had reached.

Everywhere in the school books were an essential part of the child's life and of his learning. There was no doubt in the mind of the visitor as to the quality of learning taking place in a school such as this, where children had learned to live with books in their hands.

The aim of teaching reading is to make life richer and more meaningful. Sometimes teachers make oral reading skill their goal and select material with this aim in view. They decide what the child shall read and how he shall read it. Then they wonder why these children are such poor readers when they reach the Secondary School.

If we select books with care and surround the child with material of real literary worth, if we give him time to browse and to choose what interests him to read and if we help him to enjoy it we are fostering positive reading habits which provide the sound foundation of later literacy. What we do about books at this stage should encourage the child to go on reading, and he *will* read if we make it worth his while to do so.

18

Imaginative writing

The words which a child finds most interesting are those which he has discovered himself. Helping the child to write his own words on paper shows him not only the purpose of creative writing but also helps him to understand the nature of reading. Reading and writing are two parts of a single process and develop side by side in the modern Infant School. Many children learn to read as much through their own writing as from printed books.

We all live in a world of talkers. The creative and imaginative use of words in the form of speech has developed in us naturally as part of our adjustment to an articulate society. If we can talk we have it in us to become writers and most of us employ a variety of forms of creative writing during the course of our daily lives. Letter writing is virtually universal, and as transport facilities increase so communication by written word plays an ever-increasing part in the affairs of man.

When writing to a friend most of us compose good letters, because we write in a relaxed relationship and enjoy telling our thoughts to a sympathetic person. We describe a new hat, we report an event, we express our views about pay negotiations, we tell a story about an experience. Each of these represents a form of creative writing. We have the ability to use words on paper but how many of us can weave those words into poetry, create a spell-binding story, or narrate a really vivid account of a situation? How many of us feel inhibited when it comes to the poetic and imaginative use of our own words? And, although most of us would enjoy the thrill of meeting our own words in print, we are often reluctant to admit to being the author of a poem.

The mind of the adult is rich with experience, but most of us feel inadequate when expressing ourselves on paper. Somewhere along the line we could have been helped to translate the material in our minds into some really artistic form, but instead, what happened? The teacher said: 'Be creative for twenty minutes, starting now at half-past nine on Monday morning'. She gave us comprehension exercises or instructed us to fill in the missing words. We had exercises in punctuation and grammar, and we were afraid to try new words in case we spelled them incorrectly; we didn't talk much about our words, and the right word constantly evaded us; we were given a stilted and inadequate handwriting style and our thoughts stumbled through physical frustration; finally, our painstaking efforts were scored with red pencil until we revolted against them. Our ultimate goal was to write answers to examination questions. We learned to cling to what was safe and would look neat and tidy, and imagination remained dormant and became stunted.

A child finds a toad in the garden. He notices its queer skin and its bulging eyes; he watches it leap. He must tell someone about it, and he'll talk to anyone who will listen – his mother, his teacher, his friend. If there is no one around he will talk to himself. He may try to draw or paint all he has experienced. This is his material for creative writing, and with some help he can put what he has to say on paper using the words he has spoken, and his experiences will be extended and preserved.

Some children come into school scarcely able to make

recognisable shapes on paper, some even find difficulty in holding and using a pencil. Some children by the age of seven or eight are writing poetry and 'novels' of about seven or eight hundred words. Helping the child to write spontaneously and independently of help from an adult is a magnificent feat of skill which many teachers accomplish. Most children will continue to require some assistance for many years after they leave the Infant School.

In order to write imaginatively the child must have something to write about, a wealth of words with which to express his ideas, the tool of handwriting, the opportunity to write when he feels creative, and time to finish his work. These are the things which the teacher can provide.

Many children begin to write before they can read. Their childish scribble may include the odd letter or number symbol, or even whole words and parts of sentences. Sometimes the child will tell the onlooker what his 'writing' says, or alternatively he may ask to have it translated for him. At a very early age a child is anxious to express himself on paper, and his writing, picture-making and reading are part of his effort to communicate. He is very proud of the results of his efforts and will show them to an adult, hoping for approval. His emotional satisfaction here is highly important in establishing his later attitude. A child who sees his scribble consigned to the fire or waste-paper basket may lose respect for his work and his enthusiasm will wilt.

David loved the new climbing apparatus. He fetched a plain paper book from the writing-corner and filled it with coloured pictures of himself using the apparatus. He chattered to his teacher about his pictures and she wrote a simple caption beneath each: 'I like the ladder best', 'I can swing from the long rope', and so on. David read the captions. He then went over them with his pencil. As he reached the end of the book, he copied the captions beneath his teacher's writing. He then wrote THE END independently.

Michael's favourite toy was his aunt's old typewriter. He typed messages and left them for parents and relatives to read. He could type words before he could write them and the typewriter was a tool he could use to help him transfer his thoughts to paper.

Sometimes the actual writing is done by the teacher as an extension of the child's speech. The child uses the teacher as a tool. Elizabeth loved poetry, and poetic ideas often sprang to her mind. At six she found handwriting difficult and made frequent use of her teacher. 'I've got another story,' she would exclaim. 'Will you write it for me, Mrs Brown? . . . "The rain drops, the silver drops on a spider's cobweb".' By the time she was seven her academic skill had caught up with her imagination.

We can enrich a child's vocabulary and stimulate his desire to write in a number of ways. We do it directly by introducing a child to a wide variety of experiences which make him want to talk and, later, to record. This does not mean we must be constantly organising ambitious expeditions. Children are just as excited about the beetle scurrying out of the crack in the pavement as they are about the elephant in the zoo.

Indirect stimulation comes from introducing children to the best that literature can offer. We choose stories that are told well, using good vocabulary. Our selection of poems includes as much 'real' poetry as jingle or verse, for the work of the artist inspires and provides a good pattern. We cultivate in our children an appreciation of the beauty of words and the exquisite use of them. We want them to capture something of the magic and wonder evident in Eleanor Farjeon's poem, *What is Poetry?*

> What is poetry? Who knows?
> Not the rose, but the scent of the rose;
> Not the sky, but the light of the sky;
> Not the fly, but the gleam of the fly;

Not the sea, but the sound of the sea;
Not myself, but what makes me
See, hear and feel, something that prose
Cannot; and what it is, who knows?

We encourage children to collect words – about light, for instance. The language of light is almost poetry:

Ray, beam, gleam, moonbeam, dawn, aurora,
Spark, flash, blaze, flame,
Shine, glitter, twinkle, flare, shimmer,
Scintillating, translucent,
Transparent, limpid, glossy, iridescent.

We have considered the importance of the teacher's own speech in helping the child with his words. Many of our children come from homes where speech is slovenly, where conversation may be confined to a series of ejaculations, where swearing and undesirable expressions are used as often as good English. The first good speech a child hears spoken personally to him may be that of his teacher. Because she is such an important person to him he will take note of her speech and try to use it himself. He will find that there are more widely understood ways of saying 'summat' (something), 'on t' road' (on the road), and that good speech is pleasing to the ear.

His teacher will help him to use his words accurately and convey his meaning precisely. When he says that the sun has 'sucked up' the water from the wet playground, she will give him the word 'evaporate'. She will encourage him to perceive with care, for accurate observation is conducive to good writing. What he touches he will learn to feel, what he hears he will learn to listen to and what he looks at he will learn to watch. Then his mind will receive a rich store of information from which to weave his thoughts.

Writing materials should always be available in the classroom, and if they are attractive they will encourage the child to record his thoughts and feelings. There is some itch in man which drives him to make his mark on a plain surface, and the teacher who provides an assortment of home-made books with coloured card covers will have as many candidates to use them as she has books.

Unlined paper will give the child a surface free of restrictions when his attempts to write are immature and unformed. Thick pencils are easier to handle for the child whose finer muscles are undeveloped. Crayons for illustration, boxes of pictures, equipment for making small books quickly as they are needed – all are part of the writing-table.

In many schools children are taught script print as a preliminary to handwriting, but a number of schools have adopted a simple cursive style, such as that devised by Marion Richardson, as a suitable beginner's tool. This style has the advantage of being a natural development of the child's early scribble, and by the time the child is seven and his ideas flow a cursive style enables him to set them down quickly and legibly. It is, moreover, a style which provides the foundation for an adult hand; there is no switch from script print to handwriting on entering the Junior School. A cursive hand may take a little longer to acquire in the early stages, but it provides the child with an adequate tool by the time his thoughts are beginning to take shape.

Sometimes the craft of handwriting is taught as an art form not necessarily connected with what the child wishes to put down on paper. Marion Richardson recommended the teaching of her style through a pattern approach with a brush. Most schools help the child to acquire his hand as part of the effort to express his ideas on paper. He is given the tool as he goes along, but emphasis may be placed on the handwriting itself from time to time as, for instance, when he compiles an anthology of 'Poems We Love'.

Much depends on the good model provided by the teacher. Children are faithful imitators and will take care to reproduce the teacher's characteristic style. Few schools nowadays expect children to fill copy books. Copying from the blackboard is also unusual. Indeed for the young child the problem of visualising and then reproducing blackboard copy renders this a very difficult exercise. Copy beneath a good model, with some help for individual difficulties, is perhaps the most appropriate way to acquire the tool. Handwriting is only a means to an end, not an end in itself. The study of handwriting as an art-form can come later, if required.

When children first try to put down their thoughts on paper we expect immature standards in appearance, spelling and punctuation. Our first aim is to encourage free translation of ideas into written form. As their writing matures, children can understand the need for accuracy, legibility and punctuation, if what they have written is to be read by others.

In the very early stages the teacher provides the child with a copy of what he wants to say. Very soon the child will try to write some words without the aid of the teacher. Some children are very independent, and although they may write queer versions of the words they want to use it is advisable to encourage them in their independence. Each child has a book of plain pages in which the teacher can write the words he cannot spell. These are simple at first, but the child soon sees a purpose in organising them and eventually in the use of alphabetical order. It is at this point, for most children, that the alphabet makes sense and the letters can be memorised in traditional order. In time the child learns how to use printed dictionaries, and there are on the market many well-illustrated dictionaries suitable for use by beginners.

Reading aloud what he has written helps a child to see the purpose of full stops, capital letters and commas. The teacher can point out, from a familiar story printed in a book, how to indicate dialogue. When a child's book is given a place of honour alongside printed books on the library shelves, it becomes obvious to him that it must be written in a socially acceptable form. The writing of good

Children also composed their own prayers for school service:

'Dear God help me to be good and always kind to ather pepol and when I grow up help me to be kind to my children. I have always wonted a little baby but I cannot have one becus I am too young.'

'Dear God I am thanking you for sending baby Jesus to Mary because on Christmas day it is Jesus birthday and I hope Mary is glad when it is Jesus birthday and God sent baby Jesus to Mary and Mary said thankyou to God and now we are saying thankyou to you.'

By the time they are seven many children are writing stories of considerable length. Imitating their long story books some children in one school wrote 'novels', arranged in chapters, built round a plot or a character and employing the accurate use of dialogue. 'The Adventures of Timothy and Tim on a Bicycle' and 'The Odd-Job Man' were the titles of two of these.

When we set so-called English exercises or composition, we underestimate children's ability, we are crippling their imagination. If a teacher is to liberate in her children the power to communicate imaginatively what they think and feel, her first job is to inspire in them a sense of the beauty and majesty of words.

19

Helping the child to become literate

Modern society seems obsessed by the desire for premature development. Any project which promises earlier performance gets a hearing. Many parents and teachers sincerely believe that if they force a child into doing at five what he would grow into at six, then the child benefits, and they are seen to be more efficient as educators. All that we know now about the significance of maturation has little effect on this belief when it comes to the teaching of reading. Inability to recognise printed words at an early age is regarded as proof of the failure of the educational system. We rarely hear criticism against the school in which children's reading skill is precocious and ahead of their understanding.

As adults who inherit a literate environment we want our children to acquire skill in reading as soon as possible so that they can benefit from their heritage. This is right and we must do everything we can to encourage the child's literary development, but we want him to develop fully and not merely seem to develop.

Some children develop quickly and are capable of reading long before they come into school. The frequently held concept of reading readiness occurring at six and a half needs to be exploded. A child may be three and a half chronologically or he may be eight, and the fact that he reaches the stage early or late is not always dependent on his intellectual capacity. This particular ability can ripen at stages which vary considerably between individual children.

In recent years people genuinely concerned with helping children to become literate have promoted schemes which claim to reduce the problem of word recognition and enable the child to read earlier. We will consider the more popular of these schemes. We will also consider more generally ways in which we can encourage literacy in our children.

Glenn Doman was a member of a team of American doctors and educators working to help children who suffered from brain injuries. They realised that children, even those suffering from brain damage, could be trained at a very early age to recognise printed words, provided the print was large enough. Glenn Doman then turned his attention to normal children and brought out a book entitled *Teach Your Baby to Read*,[15] in which he provides parents with step-by-step instructions for training children to articulate printed words from the age of two or even younger.

Parts of Glenn Doman's argument are very soundly based. He views reading as a brain function and not as a subject to be taught in school. 'Reading language,' he says, 'is a brain function exactly as learning language is a brain function', and again: 'Everybody plus the child's environment teaches a child to understand spoken language,' and likewise, he argues, to read. We could agree also with his statement that 'all children want to absorb information about everything around them, and under the proper circumstances reading is one of these things'. He emphasises the importance of adult attitude and urges parents to keep reading a joyous experience, avoiding anxiety at all costs.

Unfortunately there are major flaws in Glenn Doman's theory and the most important of these is his misinterpretation of the term reading. All those who live close to young children know that they recognise words such as 'Esso', 'Daz', 'Woolworths', and that they can be helped in their powers of recognition by being told what these signs stand for. But children do this as part of an activity such as filling up at the petrol station, helping mother to wash up and so on, and we must not assume that to isolate the symbols from the activity and then to train children to say them on sight is the same thing as meeting the word naturally in the live situation.

Glenn Doman says that 'very young children can read, *provided* that, in the beginning, you make the print very big'. This could be a very misleading statement, for there is far, far more to the skill of reading than the remark implies.

The method of instruction prescribed by Glenn Doman seems to be based entirely on stimulus–response learning theory.[16] The child is trained to make the correct verbal response and is profusely rewarded when he does so correctly. We could train pigeons and rats in this way, although their responses would take the form of action rather than speech. Likewise, children of eighteen months to three years can be conditioned to respond. We can train them at this stage in their mental development to make the correct response each time we show them a word pattern. They will make the right noise, but it may mean little or nothing to them. As their thought-processes become more firmly structured they require more meaning in their learning and will lose interest in these elementary forms of response. Again, do we really want the six-year-old to 'enjoy the material which would normally be presented to him when he is between eight and fourteen years of age'?

Perhaps the most distressing flaw in Glenn Doman's theory is the view he takes of the child's mind. He likens the new-born baby to an empty electronic computer and talks about placing information in a child's brain. He uses the terms information and knowledge as though they were identical. We agree entirely that the child is insatiably curious and that his thirst for knowledge is boundless. But the child's knowledge is based initially on first-hand experience. Information from other sources such as books can be grafted on to what the child has discovered for himself. To say that 'the child should learn to read and thus gain access to all knowledge' is equivalent to saying that the child will know because he is told. But, and especially at this age, a book can offer only an extension of actual experience.

Glenn Doman also assumes that homes and parents deprive children of learning opportunities, that the child is kept all the time in the play-pen, and that schools are arid of experience. He seems to have a poor concept of what goes on in good homes and lively Infant Schools. He promises to the mother who instructs her two-year-old to recognise words a child who will spend most of his time absorbed in books. Do we want the child to live at second-hand in a world of books before he has lived at first-hand with soil and water and sun-warmed wind? The child, given good chances, will learn to recognise words as part of his environment. He will use them in due course to supplement his immediate experiences and as substitutes for them, but what he reads needs the foundation of meaning, which can only be laid through adequate living at first-hand during the early stages of life. There is much more to reading than recognising and articulating words which are big enough for the child to see.

Promoters of i.t.a., the initial teaching alphabet, feel that the inconsistencies of English spelling may be a major cause of failure to read, because the conventional alphabet produces books which contain confusing variants for the child to grasp. An augmented alphabet was devised by Sir James Pitman with a view to making all words phonetic. This is not a method of teaching reading, it is a medium or alphabet. The augmented alphabet consists of forty-three letters, and each letter matches a sound. The letter 'a' in the conventional alphabet stands for several sounds as in 'at', 'any', 'want', 'all', 'say', 'bath', and so forth. We need a different letter for each of these sounds.

Basically this is a good idea, and if i.t.a. were completely adopted our language would become phonic and more easily communicable to other nationalities. In order to use it as a teaching medium, however, we must translate printed material into i.t.a. This means that the child's learning to read is limited to material which is printed in this special way and words in the child's natural environment are ignored.

It means also that formal instruction is inevitable. What we do is ask the child to ignore all printed words he finds in everyday life and direct his attention to those prepared in i.t.a. The encyclopaedia at home, Gran's bible, Auntie's letter, and the text on John's favourite cough-mixture are no longer available as reading material. The child must be trained to recognise word patterns he must later unlearn, and this is educationally most undesirable.

Again, the incentive of earlier reading is offered by the promoters of i.t.a. The child can be trained through phonetic drill to articulate words in print irrespective of whether those words mean anything to him. If a word pattern stimulates no corresponding idea in the child's mind, the fact that he can say that word can scarcely be called reading. The ability to read and write words ahead of experience has no merit at all.

A schools organiser visited a school in which i.t.a. was exclusively used in the approach to reading. She was introduced to a child of five and a half who she was told could read anything, 'even the daily newspaper fresh from the press'. The child was given an unopened copy of the *Daily Mirror*. He certainly could read it. In fact he 'read' straight across the top of all four columns!

Too often we are told of the child's *performance*. Even educational psychologists speak of how the child *performs*, as though reading were some kind of feat which a child should be trained to do. Dr Joyce Morris goes as far as to suggest that children in the Infant School should be trained to read 'at least mechanically'. Can we wonder that children grow to mistrust the printed word?

While the alphabet in general use in our country remains irregular, material printed will frequently remain non-phonetic, and phonic media such as i.t.a., which produces phonic material, will involve us in mechanical methods of teaching because they isolate the child's material from his everyday life. What happens where the majority of children are concerned is that they learn the material presented by the teacher alongside material presented by the general environment. Fortunately the child defeats attempts made by adults to deprive him of his right to learn from the best in word usage. Unless we lock away all traditional literature, write and read our letters in secret, veil all interesting advertisements and switch off the television, we cannot stop him learning from the alphabet he has inherited. Major reform in the alphabet should be approached at adult level; the conflict between traditional and revised usage should not be inflicted on the child.

Dr Gattegno's reading scheme 'Words in Colour' has something in common with i.t.a. in that it sets out to make English phonetically regular by using colour with letter shapes to distinguish the various sounds from which words are built. A teacher operating this scheme introduces sounds in isolation and the normal stimulus of books is deliberately ruled out. The material is not even illustrated. No attempt is made to teach reading through interest and meaning, and the learning situation is completely formal. The child is limited to the phonetic material prescribed by the scheme and rote learning is practised throughout. The advantage of the scheme is that it provides the child with a complete tool, for, if he knows the sounds, he can decipher any word, whether it means anything to him or not.

In recent years attempts have been made to teach reading by programmed instruction. Material is prepared and presented in much the same way as the step-by-step procedure outlined by Glenn Doman. Programmed instruction is, in fact, an extension of textbook instruction. The unique quality of programmed learning lies in its mechanical and impersonal nature.

The idea of a reading programme is that the child works individually, through small simple steps, towards the recognition of words singly and in groups. The child can work at his own pace, independent of the teacher, and he is guaranteed success. He does not suffer from competition and feelings of failure.

A few children, for reasons beyond their control, find human relationship difficult and perhaps a barrier to learning. Such children could benefit from an impersonal approach such as programmed instruction gives. For the large majority of our children, learning to read is essentially an aspect of a child's relationship with adults or sometimes with especially gifted children. Providing his mistakes are not too numerous and failure is not too severe, occasional lack of success adds zest and challenge to the exploration of the printed word. To share this adventure with someone the child loves brings joy to the experience and helps to develop healthy attitudes towards literature in later life.

Some teachers develop ideas of their own and devise apparatus, work-books and games as a reading scheme in itself or as an aid to an existing scheme. Games which centre mainly round the idea of word recognition from flash cards may help a child to form a mental image of a word pattern. Generally speaking, material of this kind tests rather than teaches, and it concentrates on visual acuity.

There are logical arguments to support all these approaches to reading. In each there is much that is commendable and teachers and parents will give them careful consideration. Educators of young children are in a position to evaluate the many suggestions made to them. It is they who will decide what is of value in helping children, what they will use, and how they will use it. At all costs they must resist the pressure of promoters, however sincere, and often of public opinion. Logical arguments readily persuade adults, but the logic of children does not run along adult lines.

Sometimes interesting schemes and attractively produced material enthuse teachers. Their enthusiasm is conveyed to the children they teach and the response of these children is gratifying. Where learning to read is concerned, as with most learning, the person who helps matters far more than the methods and material she uses. Either directly or indirectly the child must learn his language from adults. How he feels about those adults and how they treat him make the difference between effective learning and failure.

Some children can and will learn to read long before they come into school. If they can learn at the age of three and enjoy reading as part of their exploration of life around them, then we should help them. We should not, however, consider these children necessarily more favoured than the child who reads later. We should avoid that glow of pride for the child who reads at four and the inclination to extend only tepid praise for the skill of his five-year-old brother in making a picture or in swimming.

The most encouraging thing we can do about helping children to become literate is to make sure they meet and enjoy good literature. Stories are perhaps the greatest means of communication between man and man. They provided him with his first literature and they play the leading part in our introduction of literature to the child. We tell children stories we enjoy and so convey our delight in them. We select our stories with great care and treat them as part of the child's social development.

A good story for children should be exciting and keep the child wondering what happens next. It should develop through characters the child would like to live with. It should be authentic in detail and atmosphere, packed with action and dramatic situation. It should have humour. Above all it should be well written, using words which please the child and extend his vocabulary, and with an opening which makes the listener sit up and take notice.

The story-teller's equipment consists of a voice children can listen to and personal interest which enables her to set the atmosphere before the story is told. As the story is re-created between teller and audience the child should become part of the story, so that he extends his own experiences and learns more about himself as he enters into it.

The story is of intrinsic value, and telling stories primarily for the moral they are intended to convey can be a misuse of this mode of communication.

While only the best is good enough for children, this does not exclude the teacher's own creative efforts. The teacher who, knowing her children well, can create her own story and let them share in creating one to their own taste and mood has an excellent means of helping children to understand the uses of their own language. These stories can take their place amongst the stories of good writers and, from time to time, the stories of great writers. Folk stories, legends, ballads and parables are all immortalised because they contain an authentic core. Their vigour vitalises literature. The child needs his bedtime tales, but if he is to develop good taste in literature he must be given every chance to experience the work of recognised masters, particularly during the introductory years.

20

Problems associated with the teaching of reading

We have considered reading as part of the child's heritage and as a development of his speech. We have seen how the majority of our children, in spite of the various ways adults go about the teaching of reading, grow gradually and naturally into the use of words on paper. Some gain skill sooner than others, but we hope most children will make a start by the time they are seven and will be reasonably confident by the age of nine. Our educational system is designed around this assumption.

Very few children are incapable of learning to read, but each child has his own pace and a large percentage of our children experience considerable difficulty in learning to recognise printed words until they are about eight or nine. Most children need sympathetic help during the first two years in their Junior School; some need help all the way.[17]

Many children on leaving the Infant School are able to recognise quite a wide range of word patterns and attach meaning to printed words when they see them. Even so, these more able children have not completed the process. Learning to read doesn't happen at one particular time. It is a continuous experience with its roots in the child's first days, or even hours, of life, and we continue throughout life to acquire further skill in it.

Sometimes the teacher of a less able eight-year-old child blames the Infant School for not having done its job. This attitude is not likely to help and the child may feel he has committed a crime. He is often very anxious to read and is every bit as frustrated as the teacher when he fails to make any progress.

The term 'problem' associated with the teaching of reading is used to denote inability on the part of the child to acquire the skill of recognising words in print. We shall in this chapter consider the causes which delay development of the skill. We shall also consider precocious performance, for many of us have witnessed the detrimental effects of premature reading skill on the child.

It is at the Secondary School stages that we can assess the incidence of non-readers. One enquiry in the West Riding found 1·73 per cent of Secondary age children in this class. Of these, 0·99 were boys and 0·74 were girls, so that being born a boy is the first mistake a child can make. Children experienced difficulty for one or more of the following reasons: mental weakness, illness and absence from school, speech defects, poor home circumstances, and nervousness. The possibilities of faulty teaching and poor facilities in school were not mentioned.

These figures suggest that in spite of extra help given to those children who find reading a problem not all of our children acquire the skill during their school education. During the Second World War reading classes for men in the Forces were highly popular and successful. These were men motivated by their need to communicate with home. They proved that they could learn to read. Why didn't they do so in school?

A consideration of the difficulties which faced some individual children may help to elucidate the nature of the problems which hinder non-readers.

At the age of four, Eric developed a tubercular hip. He spent the next twelve years in hospital and for much of that time he had to lie on his back with his leg suspended in a frame. Occasionally he was allowed to go home for a few days, but his parents were poor and he was rarely taken anywhere exciting. In his condition even the hospital school could do very little and he reached the age of fifteen unable to read or write. The local authority then provided two hours per week individual tuition, in the hope that Eric would be equipped to cope when he was ready to leave the hospital and take his place in society.

His teacher realised from the start that easy reading material of the commercially produced type was useless. Not only was the content childish, it referred to experiences he had never had. Even simple words such as 'lake', 'race', 'market', or 'boat' conjured a weak image in Eric's mind or none at all. The only words which meant much to him were 'ceiling', 'nurse', 'bed', 'sheets', 'injections', and so on, and his teacher made him books using these words and such ideas as he might meet on radio programmes, which were his only contact with the world.

As the first excitement of the teacher's visits wore off, Eric's efforts diminished. He had few responsibilities, his life was ordered for him, he had no ambition apart from leaving the hospital and living at home. His release brought disillusionment. Neighbouring children tormented him about his crutches. The teacher tried to continue his lessons by inviting him to her home or by visiting him in his. Again children teased him about learning to read at sixteen. Eric gradually lost even the shreds of desire to make the effort. He could recognise the right bus, pay his fare, and spend the meagre money he earned at the clerical job he'd been found. What else mattered?

The odds against Eric becoming a skilful reader were great. He was not intellectually strong to begin with and his unfortunate circumstances and limited environment did nothing to promote his intellectual development. He had few words with which to read because few words had been given him, and those he had lacked the meaning which results from experience. Attempts to help him overcome his difficulties came too late. Most important of all, he lacked incentive; there was no inner power to drive him into using his limited resources effectively. Eric's aspirations were so low that learning to read seemed purposeless.

At the best of times Timothy's hearing was not good. When he had a cold he was practically deaf. At the age of seven he had made little progress with reading and had begun to stutter. Timothy was quite intelligent, but lack of success in his work made him feel less able than others and he had little confidence in himself. He was provided with a hearing aid, and an understanding teacher gave him small jobs which made him feel important and responsible. He became a person who counted in the classroom and this gave him confidence. His stutter disappeared and his reading began to develop.

Jane was a disruptive element in the school from the start. Her home background was a very disturbed one, with mother admitted to a mental hospital at varying intervals. June often wandered from home and when she returned she was beaten by her father. What she most needed was a calm, stable atmosphere, yet she destroyed every attempt on the part of her teacher to provide it. She was not unintelligent, but her speech was slovenly and she was unable to concentrate for more than a few minutes at a time. If she was left alone with a book she would tear it up.

June arrived in school one morning with terrible weals on her back and thighs. The teacher persuaded people in authority to investigate and June was eventually placed in a home by the local authority. She showed signs of responding to the patient care of the people in charge of her and she became more amenable in school. She made a number of scrap-books and started to paint, but there was still much she needed before she could be helped to recognise printed words. She left the Infant School virtually a non-starter.

Roderick's was a very different problem. He came from a professional home and his mother had him reading to visitors by the age of four. Before entering school he could 'read' any daily newspaper, information printed on bus tickets, even the V.D. notices in toilets. When asked a question, however, he would stutter or fall silent.

On his first day in school Roderick made for the woodwork bench. He refused to go near the book-corner or to make any books; the word 'book' alone evoked an emotional reaction. He spent most of his time working with his hands and adding forbidden words to his vocabulary. His teacher began to worry about his attitude to books and reading, wondering whether he had turned against them for life.

One day a child brought a rabbit to school and asked Roderick to help him make a hutch for it. Roderick's skill in woodwork enabled the two boys to produce a very creditable home for the rabbit. The headmistress seized the opportunity. 'Other people would like to make a fine hutch like yours,' she encouraged him. 'Could you put some instructions into this big scrap-book in my room?'

Roderick consented, but his instructions took the form of pictures. 'You draw well,' the headmistress told him, 'but the pictures don't tell anyone by themselves how to make the hutch. You must explain them.' Roderick added suitable notes to the pictures. This was his first book work since he entered school. Gradually he discovered a new delight in books and the joy of reading was opened to him.

From these examples we could define a number of reasons for reading disability. Physical causes are perhaps the most obvious. Defective vision or hearing and speech defects mean that the child is not physically equipped to read. Poor general health and malnutrition mean that he lacks the vitality required to tackle a difficult job. Illness and absence from school deprive the child of the chance of a good reading environment, unless his home is well endowed. An intelligent child in a literate home, on the other hand, may develop the skill when he is ill because there are fewer alternative interests when he is confined to bed.

The child with a poor home background is handicapped in a number of ways. His experiences and consequently his vocabulary are restricted, his attitude to books is undeveloped, he lacks the support of parents, who may be apathetic or indifferent like the mother who refused to let her child wear glasses in order to avoid the responsibility of looking after them.

Less obvious and more difficult to remedy are psychological causes. Anxiety, emotional disturbance, negative emotional attitudes such as resentment, apathy or inferior feelings, and Roderick's urge to resist parental pressure all take time to develop and time to break down.

Much always depends on the provision made by the school, and most important of all is the attitude of the teacher and the approach she uses. It is from these same factors that remedies for the child's disability can be found.

Anxiety is perhaps the greatest handicap to a child where reading is concerned, and anxiety on the part of the child is generally caused by the anxiety of parents or teacher. Nowadays parental anxiety tends to increase. It may be that parents feel guilty because television in the home means that they do less reading. In spite of its popularity television has not yet been accepted as a completely desirable medium in society. Why is reading approved of and television disapproved of? Parents watch television, but compensate by putting extra pressure on their children to achieve literacy.

Teachers are sensitive to this pressure on the part of parents. Many share the parents' mistakenly logical view and firmly believe that the sooner the child articulates words the more likely he is to become academically sound. Skill in reading is a status symbol and must be achieved no matter what the costs are to the child. We have still many parents and teachers, even local inspectors and HMIs, who assess the success of an Infant School on the facility with which a child reads aloud the printed word.

Much of this anxiety is due to the unfortunate effects of being unable to read in modern society. In our existing system of education the slow reader in the Junior School gets left behind. As the gap widens between his achievement and that of his friends, the child loses confidence and his attitude to his work deteriorates. Eventually he loses the desire to try. The more intelligent the child is, the more sensitive he is to failure, and his intelligence may go unrecognised by selective procedure when crucial selective tests are given.

Anxiety on the part of parent or teacher may prevent him from recognising the true cause of failure. For instance, a child who appears slow to learn may just be late, rather than slow, to learn. George was a quiet, dreamy child. He was readily absorbed in watching a bee plunder a flower for honey or a bricklayer shaping the corner of a wall. He would spend hours dismantling a clock or fashioning a boat from balsawood. He loved to listen to stories or poetry, and would enjoy turning the pages of a book, but writing or reading words on paper had little appeal until he was nearly eight. By the age of nine he was devoted to books and was quickly caught up in the magic of their contents. We would have spoilt reading for George if we had tried to hurry him.

Sometimes a child suffers from word-blindness, or dyslexia. He may be intelligent, come from a good home, show no sign of emotional disturbance, physical disability or brain-damage, and yet be quite unable to recognise word patterns. A dyslexic child cannot remember the shape of words. If he tries to write a word the letters appear in the wrong order, or he may write the word backwards.

The causes of dyslexia are not fully understood,[18] but a number of eminent personalities have been afflicted. Keats found spelling and reading a problem. Picasso never mastered the sequence of the alphabet. Hans Andersen was believed to be word-blind. There are about 75,000 dyslexic children of school age in our country. Most of them are boys, and a centre for treatment has been established in Gray's Inn Road, London, under the direction of Dr Bannatyre. Here, interest in reading is awakened by methods similar to those described in this book. Dyslexic children must be given help before they are nine, otherwise they cannot benefit from school education.

Such children are frequently misunderstood. The parent who knows his child is intelligent is disappointed by his failure to read, and this disappointment is quickly conveyed to the child, who feels that he has let his parents down. A teacher may think an intelligent dyslexic is lazy or defiant or making a monkey of her. If he is capable, why does he remain indifferent to her attention? The child's problem is increased when such a situation develops.

What happens to the children who fail to make the grade? Often they are singled out and given extra doses of the medicine which has already failed. The practice of reading is isolated from other activities and word recognition becomes a drill, distasteful in spite of efforts to ginger it up.

Children rarely benefit from being treated apart from the group. It is distressing to find head teachers who seem to think that their main contribution as the leading teacher in the school is to hear slow-learning readers stumble over printed words. The child may appreciate her kindly attempts to help him, but the image of her which he retains in later years is scarcely that of an inspired teacher.

The gifted reader may also need sympathy and special help. It is tempting for parents to exploit a young child's intellect. The prodigy is a credit to his parents and it takes a very unselfish parent to resist showing off his feats to their friends. Intelligent children are easy to teach, anxious to please, and sensitive to what is required of them. They acquire words quickly and, because they are intelligent, may grasp the meaning of a word at second hand from an adult before experience has had time to prepare the ground. The words they are encouraged to say and read may have insecure conceptual foundations. Reading then becomes a circus act performed before an approving audience.

Joanna was able to read fluently when she entered school. Already books dominated her life. She would rather read about soil than play with it. She lived more in the world of print than in the real world and was impatient with children who didn't understand what she said to them. She knew less about other children than was known by an unintelligent child from an underprivileged home. She preferred the safe world of her books to the hazards and adventure of making friends. She had to be weaned away from her books and encouraged to play. Eventually 'dressing-up' caught her imaginative interest and it was through spontaneous dramatic play that she learned to communicate with others and so learned to enjoy a measure of normal childhood. Even so, her parents felt she was wasting her time and looked for the day when she could 'go into the Junior School and do something worth while'.

Problems associated with the teaching of reading stem from many aspects of the child's total personal pattern.[19] We cannot consider them in isolation. The more deeply we consider them, the more aware we become of the integrated nature of the child's learning. Learning to read is an inseparable part of the child's whole development. It depends as much on the stage a child has reached in his awareness of his surrounding world as it does on the material and help we provide. The successful acquisition of the skill depends on the harmonious relationship between physical and psychological systems.

A child in our society grows up in a world of words. Those

words come to have meaning because they are part of his living. Problems begin to arise when we try to isolate printed words and treat them as things apart instead of treating them as one aspect of communication. Much of what takes place in some schools is little more than practising the skill of word recognition. When the learning is active and vital very little time need be spent on word analysis and practising. 'Hearing children read' as a regular drill may assure the teacher that the child can recognise word patterns, but it does little to further his reading skill. The *use* the child can make of words in print is much more a measure of his comprehension than mere articulation can ever be.

The argument that the child likes someone to hear him read is often quoted in support of the practice. A child will do much to secure the approval of adults and direct their precious attention towards himself. A child knows that he is assured of attention if he waves a reader in front of his teacher, headmistress, inspector, or other visitor to the school. He knows that few adults will resist this approach. His sense of achievement should not depend on completing one book after another. Joy in the content of books is the real reward of a skill mastered. Adult attitudes which foster these modes of behaviour in children do not help solve problems but rather help make them.

When Trevor came into school at the age of five, he had not started to read in spite of attempts made at home to help him. He was an intelligent boy, well aware of the anxiety of his parents. He saw a number of children reading and obviously enjoying the books in the classroom. Trevor settled down with a book and with one eye on his teacher simulated the skill of the older children. He made sure that his teacher 'saw him reading' several times a day, but if another child came to share his book he shut it up and put it away. It was some weeks before his teacher was able to free Trevor sufficiently from parental anxiety and enable him to get absorbed in

141

picture-making and painting and in the exploration of materials which would lay the foundation for his later reading skill.

Young children are very dependent on adults, particularly on those they love. The attitude of parents and teachers to anything they do is of supreme importance. Where the teaching of reading is concerned the right relationship between child and adult is far more influential than the approach, the methods, or the material used.

Conclusion : parents and teachers

The education of the child is the joint responsibility of parents and teachers. In the development of language the essential nature of this partnership is clearly perceived. A child is favoured when he shares language with parents and teachers who are alive to the joy of their mother tongue and who are sensitive to the vital spirit of language in all its diversified forms. A child will learn to love and enjoy English because those who teach him love and enjoy it.

Parents are directly responsible for providing their child with the essential tool of his learning, and if a child's home has failed to equip him well verbally he faces school with a handicap which may very well cripple him personally as well as intellectually. Teachers have few illusions about the help they can give. Verbal foundations must be well laid during the early stages of development, and even the most articulate and imaginative teacher finds great difficulty in developing the child's linguistic skills when those foundations are weak.

In our society we do not leave the task of rearing children to parents alone. Nor do we believe in a system which delegates this essential responsibility to the State alone. The whole of our educational procedure is based on our belief in a balance of responsibility between parents and teachers. Before we ever plan for the child within the system we should do well to consider the true nature of this partnership. The Plowden Committee were clear-minded about this and made it an important issue in their Report:

'One of the essentials for educational advance is a closer partnership between the two parties to every child's education . . . Homes and schools interact continuously' (102). 'It has long been recognised that education is concerned with the whole man: henceforth it must be concerned with the whole family' (129).

The child learns more about language in the four or five years before entering school than he will ever learn again within the same span of time. What he learns about language in all its diversity must be grafted during his school years on to the language he already has. It is no good expecting a child to learn about reading or writing, about speaking or thinking, at any particular stage in his life. Parents must prepare the ground and support the growing skill in the child. Teachers must recognise the contribution of parents and show a perpetual willingness to acquaint them with what they try to do in school. Such attitudes of co-operation will indirectly reinforce all the child learns as his linguistic confidence grows.

Suggestions for further reading

An asterisk indicates a text which is probably too technical for the general reader.

Chapter 2

1 *Luria, A. R. and Yudovich, F. *Speech and the Development of Mental Processes in the Child.* Staples Press, 1959.
2 Lewis, M. M. *How Children Learn to Speak.* Harrap, 1957. *Infant Speech.* Kegan Paul, 1936.

Chapter 3

3 *Watts, A. F. *The Language and Mental Development of Children.* Chapter 2. Harrap, 1963 (1944).

Chapter 6

4 *De Cecco, John P. *The Psychology of Language, Thought and Instruction.* (Readings.) New York: Holt, Reinhart and Winston Inc., 1967. (See especially the articles by Berlyne and Piaget in Chapter 7.)
5 Isaacs, N. and Theakston, T. R. *Some Aspects of Piaget's* (London) *Work.* National Froebel Foundation, 1955.

Chapter 7

6 **Lewis, H.** *The Day is Ours*. Hutchinson, 1952. Chivers (reprint), 1962. The well-known Helen Keller is another example.

7 ***Peel, E. A.** *The Psychological Basis of Education*. (In particular Chapters 12 and 13.) Oliver & Boyd, 1956.

Chapter 9

8 **Gesell, A.** *The First Five Years of Life*. New York: Harper, 1940.
*Carmichal, Leonard (Ed.). *Manual of Child Psychology*. New York: Wiley, 1940. (Article by Dorothea McCarthy on 'Language Development in Children'.)

9 ***Watts, A. F.** (See No. 3 above.)

Chapter 11

10 *Half our Future*. HMSO., 1963.

Chapter 12

11 ***De Cecco, John P.** (See No. 4 above.) Chapter 7. Articles by Bernstein and Jensen.
Bernstein, Basil. *Educational Research*. Published for the National Foundation for Educational Research by Newnes Educational Publishing Co., 1961.

12 **Wiseman, S.** *Education and Environment*. Manchester University Press, 1964.
Douglas, J. W. B. *The Home and the School*. MacGibbon and Kee, 1964.

Chapter 14

13 **Boome, E. J.** and **Richardson, M. A.** *The Nature and Treatment of Stammering.* Methuen, 1947.
*Steen, Leopold. *Speech and Voice.* Methuen, 1938.

Chapter 15

14 ***Knoll, V. H.** and **R. P.** *Readings in Educational Psychology.* The Macmillan Co. of New York, 1962. (Paper No. 8: 'When Should Children Begin to Read?' M. V. Morphett and C. Washburne.)

Chapter 19

15 **Doman, Glenn.** *Teach Your Baby to Read.* Jonathan Cape, 1965.
16 **Skinner, B. F.** **Cumulative Records.* Methuen, 1962.
*Verbal Behaviour. New York: Appleton, 1957.

Chapter 20

17 *Scottish Council for Educational Research. *Studies in Reading.* Volume 1. ULP, 1948.
18 *Children and their Primary Schools.* (Para. 590). HMSO, 1967.
19 **Morris, J. M.** *How Far Can Reading Backwardness be Attributed to School Conditions?* Address given to International Reading Association, 1964; published in *The First International Reading Symposium* (Ed. J. Downing), Cassell, 1966.

Index

books, child's use of 110–12; displaying 93 109–10; history of children's 101–2; illustrated 105; in home and school 92; introducing the child to 109; making 28; selecting 106–108

class differences, effect of 73–6
communication, as total experience 31; creative work as 28; play as a mode of 28; range of 27
conversation, of children 29–30
counting 53
creative work 28–9

dictionaries, use of 119
Doman, Glenn 124–6 129
dyslexia 138–9

environment, as stimulus to development 42–3 59–60
examinations, assessment by 36–7 70
exploration, and survival 11

grammar 114 119–20

handwriting 118–19
home, effect of linguistically deprived 75–7

instruction 62–3
intelligence tests 70
i.t.a. 126–8

listening, as part of speech development 84–6; joy of 27–8 86–7 90

Newsom Report 68
non-readers, difficulties of 133–40

parental anxiety 141–2
parent-child relationship 17–18
personality, child's awareness of 45–7
phonetics 96
Piaget 38–9 99
play, dramatic 60–1; importance of 28
Plowden Report 60 75 144
poetry 86–7 116–17 121
pressures, in school 70
programmed learning 128–9

questions, child's use of 58 63–4

reading, aim of teaching 70–2 82 112; aloud 104 111 141; and writing 113–14; as a status symbol 138; continuous process of 71–2 132; disability 133 136–7; early 130; early aids to 103–4; gifted 139–40; joy of 105; late 138; problems associated with 133–40; readiness to read 95–6 123; remedial 139
reading schemes 97–9 108 124–30
reasoning, growth of 39; verbal 59
recording, in words 65–6

scribblings 50–1
self-expression: crying 26; laughter 27; physical movement 28
self-idea, development of 46–9

speech, and personality 56; as communication 26; beginnings of 10–13 16–17; child's need of 54; developing good 19–20 60; drama and 60–1; expressive use of 58; faulty 86; function of 15; influence of home background on 18–20 73–8; joy of 17; practising 57; stages in development of 19; teacher's 60 80 90

stories, value of 86–7 130–1

symbols, developing use of 50; discriminating between 51; learning to use 33; mathematical 53; personal meaning of 52; range of man's 32 35; use in Infant Schools 34–5

talking, in school 29–31 84

tape-recorder, as aid to good speech 87–8

Teach Your Baby to Read 124

telephone, as aid to good speech 88–9

television programmes 89–90

thought, development of 33 38–9; Piaget's view of 38–9; words and 21 41–2

vocabulary, building the child's 16 23 54 80–1 116

words, exploration and 13–14; expressive use of 64–5; in action 83; in education 36 62–3; in print 69–70 81 91 95–6; living nature of 25; meaning of 11–14 21–3; playing with 66–7 99; pleasure of 66; recognition of 98–9; significance of 9 68 79; thought and 21 41–2

'Words in Colour' (Dr. Gattegno's reading scheme) 128

writing, letter- 113–14; imaginative 115; materials 117–18

LB
1139
.L3
Y3
1973

Yardley, Alice.
    Exploration and language. New
York, Citation Press, 1973 [c1970]
    150 p. 19 cm. (Her Young child-
ren learning)

    Bibliography: p. 145-147.

    1. Children—Language. I. Title.

LB1139.L3Y3 1973   372.6   73-160633
ISBN 0-590-07330-3   MARC

Library of Congress
03860 01 754073   8021

© THE BAKER & TAYLOR CO.